LAGRANGE AND BIBLICAL RENEWAL

CONTRIBUTORS

RT. REV. JOHN M. T. BARTON, D.D., F.S.A. *Ancien élève* of the *École biblique de Jérusalem;* Consultor to the Pontifical Biblical Commission; President (1952) of the *Society for Old Testament Study;* frequent contributor to *The Clergy Review.*

RT. REV. PATRICK W. SKEHAN, S.T.D., S.S.L. Head of the Department of Semitics and Egyptian Languages and Literatures at Catholic University; Consultor to the Biblical Commission; President (1946-47) of the *Catholic Biblical Association;* Director (1955-56) of the *American School of Oriental Research* (Jerusalem).

REV. EUGENE H. MALY, S.T.D., S.S.D. A *peritus* at Vatican Council II; President (1962-63) of the *Catholic Biblical Association;* Editor of *The Bible Today;* Professor of Scripture at Mt. St. Mary's Seminary, Norwood, Ohio.

REV. BRUCE VAWTER, C.M., S.S.D. President (1961-62) of the *Catholic Biblical Association;* author of *A Path Through Genesis* and *The Conscience of Israel;* Editor of the *Catholic Biblical Quarterly.*

REV. GEORGE T. MONTAGUE, S.M., S.T.D. Graduate of the *Université de Fribourg;* author of *Maturing in Christ;* Head of Graduate Department at St. Mary's University, San Antonio, Texas.

REV. SEBASTIAN BULLOUGH, O.P., M.A. (Cantab.). Author of *The Church in the New Testament, St. Paul and the Apostolic Writings, Roman Catholicism,* and articles in English journals. Father Bullough teaches at the University of Cambridge.

RICHARD MURPHY, O.P., S.S.D., EDITOR

LAGRANGE
AND
BIBLICAL RENEWAL

Aquinas Institute Studies
Number 1

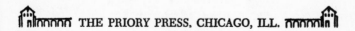 THE PRIORY PRESS, CHICAGO, ILL.

Revisores Ordinis: Augustine Rock, O.P., Bernard O'Riley, O.P. *Imprimi potest*: Gilbert J. Graham, O.P., Provincial. *Nihil obstat*: Augustine Rock, O.P., Bernard O'Riley, O.P., Censores Deputati. *Imprimatur*: Most Reverend Cletus F. O'Donnell, J.C.D., Vicar General, Archdiocese of Chicago, December 22, 1965.

Library of Congress Catalogue Number 66-17484
© Copyright 1966 by The Priory Press
2005 South Ashland Avenue, Chicago, Illinois 60608
Manufactured in the United States of America

FOREWORD Intellectual isolation inevitably leads to narrowness and sterility of thought. Scholarship flourishes where scholars are able to test evidence and compare their conclusions against those of other experts.

In no other area is the free exchange of ideas of greater importance than in the study of Holy Scripture, for no other science, physics and electronics possibly excepted, has in our day experienced so rapid an expansion of knowledge.

The vitality of the biblical movement is directly traceable to the astonishing amount of ancient materials which archaeology has recently made available to the scholar. Not only is it now often possible to reconstruct with reasonable accuracy the life of the ordinary man in biblical times, but also to know better what he and his fellows thought about religion and life in general, and the very language in which they expressed themselves. Besides, a wealth of extrabiblical material now enables the scholar to view biblical history and legislation not in a vacuum, but in the vital framework of contemporary and neighboring civilizations. God's Book belongs to *this* world.

Faced with such an embarrassment of riches, the scholar now more than ever needs to keep in touch with the work of other scholars. The lecture series begun at the *Aquinas Institute, School of Theology* was designed to maintain the free-flow of ideas between scholars and from them to students, and to educated men and women of the laity.

The series was auspiciously inaugurated (1963) on the 25th anniversary of the death of Father M. J. Lagrange, O.P., founder of the *École biblique de Jérusalem* (1890), and of its internationally famous voice, the *Revue biblique*.

Combining in himself the technical competence of the genuine scholar and the piety of a true believer, Lagrange is largely responsible for the present healthy condition of Catholic biblical studies. It might even be said that in opening his School he launched an *aggiornamento* of his own. The importance of archaeology he recognized at once, but he insisted even more on careful contact with the biblical text itself and with the original languages. The views he advanced on biblical history shocked the conservatives of his day, but his views are now seen to have been both realistic and sound.

Lagrange was a pioneer, talented, courageous, honest and fair towards opponents, a gentleman always. He contributed to the study of Scripture and to the biblical movement as a whole an example of energy and optimism, a sense of balance, and respect for both tradition and science.

It is therefore fitting that the first volume of the *Aquinas Institute Papers* be dedicated to Père Lagrange. In these pages the reader will sense something of the impact of this warrior student on his own times, and on ours.

Richard Murphy, O.P.
Aquinas Institute
Dubuque, Iowa

CONTENTS

J O H N   M.   T.   B A R T O N

1: THE DOMINICAN SCHOOL IN JERUSALEM AND OLD TESTAMENT STUDIES It was my first president at St. Edmund's College, Ware, the late Monsignor Bernard Ward, afterwards first bishop of Brentwood, who used to tell a pathetic little story about Cardinal Manning's seminary at Hammersmith which suffered from a chronic shortage of funds. It was the custom at dinner for the waiter to ask each student in turn, and in stentorian tones, "Beef or mutton, Sir?" and then to add *sotto voce*, "There's no mutton, so you'll 'ave to 'ave beef!" It is a story that occasionally has application to matters not concerned with beeves and fatlings, and this paper, which sets out to give (what we examiners are so fond of styling) some account of my Alma Mater, the Dominican School of St. Stephen, Jerusalem, and its work on behalf of Old Testament studies, may be found to be deficient in various respects. This is partly from lack of time, and partly because the subject is a big one and would require for its adequate development a more intimate knowledge of the School's various publications than I can claim to possess. I have, it is true, been a subscriber to the *Revue biblique* for nearly thirty years, and possess a set of the bound volumes that is complete from 1900 onwards. I have most of the volumes of the "Études bibliques" series issued by the School with the exception of one or two numbers, such as Père Lagrange's *Le Messianisme chez les Juifs* and Père Condamin's *Le Livre d'Isaie,* which seem now to be all but unobtainable. Still, anything resembling a full account would be a vast undertaking. Yet, since the School itself was founded seventy-five years ago (on the Feast of St. Albert the Great, November 15, 1890) and since the diamond jubilee of its principal organ, the *Revue biblique,* is long past, it may be accounted an act of *pietas* on my part to say something, however inadequately, about the École, the *Revue,* and also the founder and (for just under half a century) sustainer of both School and review, the Very Reverend Père Marie-Joseph Lagrange, that great light of the Dominican Order and of the Western Church.

I have been fortunate enough to have had many Alma Maters, all dear, all frequently in my mind whether I am seated at my desk or typewriter or standing at the altar of God. Of all these I count two most dear—the École Biblique de Saint-Étienne and, if I may so style it, the Society of Old Testament Study, whose happy and fruitful membership I have enjoyed since October, 1924, at which time I was both the first priest and the first member of my

Church to apply for admission, some seven years after its foundation in 1917. Both the School and the Society are too well known to call for any introduction, but I shall be happy if I can say anything that will, as it were, prolong the introduction of one to the other.

My own first acquaintance with the École came almost at the half-way line in the period of seventy-five years that I am attempting to survey. It was in October, 1922, after I had completed my studies for the doctorate in divinity in the Dominican faculty in Rome, that I first set eyes on that tranquil, beloved, and memory-haunted house of studies, and upon the holy and simple man who had been its founder in 1890. For two wonderful years I was a member of that lively and studious community of St. Stephen's, and I was able to savor those words quoted by the late Professor Alexander Nairne in his stimulating book *Every Man's Story of the Old Testament:* "The Bible is itself a literature, and it leads us into many various literatures, and into the society of scholars." On leaving the Holy Land in the high summer of 1924, and during all the years that have passed since then, I could make my own that dictum of Sir Ronald Storrs in his brilliant *Orientations:* "For me Jerusalem stood and stands alone among the cities of the world. There are many positions of greater authority and renown within and without the British Empire, but in a sense that I cannot explain, there is no promotion after Jerusalem."

A word may be inserted here, in anticipation, about the bibliography of my subject. There is no full life of Père Lagrange in print, and no complete history of the School. Perhaps the most generally useful of all works on the subject is that by the Belgian Dominican, Père François Braun, O.P. (an exact contemporary of mine at St. Stephen's), which is entitled *L'oeuvre du Père Lagrange*. It was published at Fribourg, Switzerland, in 1943.[1] It has the merit of listing no less than 1,786 items of the Lagrange bibliography. These include the eighteen volumes written for the "Études bibliques" series, about a dozen other books, and some 1,750 lesser writings — articles, book reviews, bulletins, and the like. There are also the Father's scanty writings about himself: that is, a few pages in his answer to Loisy's voluminous *Mèmoires,* entitled *M. Loisy et le Modernisme,*[2] and an article for the *Revue biblique* in 1915 with the title "Après vingt-cinq ans," contributed at the time in the First World War when the School had been closed and its library dispersed by the Turks. Père Louis Hugues Vincent, his pupil and close friend of nearly fifty

[1] The English version, *The Work of Père Lagrange,* adapted from the French by Richard T. A. Murphy, O.P. (Milwaukee: Bruce Publishing Co., 1963), appeared on the 25th anniversary of Père Lagrange's death.
[2] M. J. Lagrange, subtitle: *A propos des Mémoires de A. Loisy* (Paris: Editions du Cerf, 1932).

years, wrote a most illuminating article, to which I am heavily indebted, in the number of the *Revue* for July, 1938, and this he has summarized in the twenty-fourth fascicle of the *Supplément* to Vigouroux's *Dictionnaire de la Bible* (Kalt-Langdon, 1950, cols. 231-237). Then there are many details to be gleaned from the *Festschrift* published in 1934 under the title *L'oeuvre exégètique et historique du Père Lagrange,* later translated by Father Richard T. A. Murphy, O.P., as *Père Lagrange and the Scriptures,*[3] and from the *Mémorial Lagrange* volume,[4] issued in 1940, which contains two capital contributions on Père Lagrange's method of work and way of life written by Monsignor Bruno de Solages, rector of the Catholic faculty of Toulouse, and the late Abbé Joseph Chaine, professor of New Testament exegesis on the Lyons faculty.

The future founder of the School was born on March 7, 1855, at Bourg-en-Bresse in the department of Ain in southern France. His family was of Burgundian and Lyonnais stock and belonged to the old provincial bourgeoisie. His father was a notary of excellent repute, and the child received the name of Albert at his baptism. To those who knew him only as a grown man, powerfully built and full of energy even in extreme old age, it comes as a surprise to learn that he was a delicate child and needed every care

[3](Milwaukee: Bruce, 1946).
[4](Paris: Gabalda).

when he was sent for his classical studies to the minor seminary at Autun, where the teaching was exceptionally thorough. There he showed an interest in Greek that continued with him for the remainder of his life, so that, in his Jerusalem years, his favorite reading in the somnolent afternoons was frequently a Greek author. He also learned a number of modern languages with great ease, so that he was always quite at home in most of the world's best literature. (One of his last requests to me was to find him anything on Shakespeare that I could discover.) Just after he had passed his public examinations, the Franco-Prussian War broke out and he wanted to serve with the colors. His father persuaded him to stay at home since he was still very young, and later, when the son showed a desire to become a Dominican, advised him to wait a little and in the meantime to continue his legal studies. To avoid any interruption in his course, Lagrange managed to advance the time of his year's compulsory military service; in later life he always spoke with gratitude of the many lessons he had learned during that year. From 1873 until 1878 he was occupied with his legal studies, but he did not neglect Greek, and he much enjoyed all that was best in the musical and artistic life of Paris. He also did a good deal of visiting among the poor, and gave much time to a study of the chief theological and apologetic problems of the day.

On July 6, 1878, he successfully defended his thesis for the doctorate in law, and, within two months of his call to the bar, had entered the famous Sulpician house of studies at Issy-les-Moulineaux, where his chief friends were Pierre Batiffol, afterwards Monsignor Batiffol, renowned theologian and patrologist, and Henri Hyvernat, who was for many years professor of Coptic at the Catholic University of America. For a year he followed the course of philosophy, and, at the same time, developed that *gout passionné pour la parole de Dieu* for which he was always profoundly grateful to his Sulpician masters. He left Issy at the end of the summer term of 1879, and by October of that year had begun his novitiate at the Dominican house of St. Maximin near Marseilles, where, nearly sixty years later, in October 1937, about five months before his death, I visited him. He was professed on October 7, 1880, and had hardly begun his theological studies when the community at St. Maximin, with all the other Dominican friars in France, was driven into exile. The members of the St. Maximin house of studies assembled quickly in Salamanca, where a faculty of Oriental studies existed, and there Lagrange was able to continue the study of Hebrew that he had already begun at Issy with M. Hyvernat. Most of his time, naturally enough, was given over to the study of the ordinary subjects in the theology course, notably to the *Summa* of St.

Thomas Aquinas, described by the late Archbishop William Temple, in words that Lagrange would have relished, as "the most complete map ever drawn." He was ordained a priest at Zamora on December 22, 1883, and in the following July, after a brilliant examination, became a Doctor of Divinity. The moment had come when he would, in the ordinary course of events, have been sent to some faculty of higher studies, but lack of personnel obliged his superiors to put him teaching Church history and helping with the ordinary work of the ministry. The moment arrived for the return from exile, the community at Toulouse took up its old life again, and Père Lagrange, while teaching philosophy and still much occupied with pastoral work, was able to make some progress in his Near Eastern studies under the guidance of Abbé Thomas of the Catholic faculty of Toulouse. Postgraduate studies in the fullest sense, however, seemed to be remote when, quite suddenly, Père Colchen, then provincial of the Toulouse province, decided that Lagrange should be sent to Vienna to perfect his knowledge of Oriental languages. This, be it remarked, was the decision that, in due course, called into existence a properly-equipped biblical school in Jerusalem.

Now came the great months, some of the most fruitful ever known in the whole history of Oriental studies in the Christian West. Lagrange already knew something of Syriac, Arabic, and Assyrian and so was competent to begin fairly advanced studies. At Vienna, during the eighteen months alloted to him for the purpose, he studied Assyrian under David Heinrich Müller, Egyptian (both hieroglyphic and hieratic) under Professor Reinisch, and Arabic with Müller at the University and also with Professor Wahrmund at the School of Commerce. From Müller he learned, in addition, a great deal about rabbinic exegesis and the use of the Mishnah. In later years he was accustomed to bewail his incompetence in the matter of Semitic languages. At least he was never at a loss in the most difficult texts written in Hebrew, Aramaic, and the allied dialects of the Northwestern group, and, in regard to the other Semitic languages, he was not at the mercy of anybody who happened to have specialized in them. To his mind, in general, one could apply a phrase that occurs in the *Times'* obituary notice of Professor F. C. Burkitt: "The pages of the encyclopedia were ever open."

In the midst of his studies at Vienna, while he was already beginning to have some ideas about his future work as a professor of Scripture at Toulouse, he was informed by Père Colchen that he was being lent to the Dominican house in Jerusalem, so that he might found a biblical school there. Up to that time he knew little, if anything, about any house in Jerusalem, but he was soon to discover that the old slaughter house in

the Holy City had come into the hands of the Dominican Order, and had been fitted up to house a few invalid Fathers, whose superior, Père Matthieu Lecomte,
had recently died. But, as regards a house of studies,
there were no professors, no students, no library, and
no money to build any additions to the very cramped
quarters provided by the former *abattoir*. Jerusalem was
a city which, in those days under the Turkish regime,
did nothing to encourage any suspicion of higher studies. Rumor had it that the climate was an impossible
one for students—too cold in winter and pitilessly hot
in summer. Indeed, it was at one time suggested that
the students would have to be prepared to live under-
ground, in what might now be styled deep air-raid
shelters, lighted by gas and artificially ventilated, during
the six hotter months of the year. In the face of all
these discouragements, Lagrange asked for and obtained
leave to spend a further term at Vienna in order to
complete his work on Eastern languages, and then, in
the spring of 1890, he set out for Palestine. On March
9, two days after his thirty-fifth birthday and precisely
nel mezzo del cammin di nostra vita (as, traditionally,
was Dante when he began to write the *Divina Com-
media*) he was, in Père Vincent's phrase, "so to speak,
cast ashore on the inhospitable beach at Jaffa, in a
heavy sea." After a night in the hermitage at Amwas,
he arrived on the tenth, to become part of the community housed amid the ruins of the ancient sanctuary

erected on the traditional site of St. Stephen's martyr-dom.

The warm welcome he received from the Fathers could not conceal from him the fact that prospects for the foundation of a biblical school were, as he had foreseen, extremely bleak. Yet, there were compensations. A recently passed French statute offered substantial benefits to students who took up residence in a missionary country before their twentieth year. In the event, Lagrange was able to gather together a number of promising young men who were privileged to make their first contact with Oriental studies while they were still in their teens. And then, already, within a few days of his arrival, the enchantment of the land had taken fast hold on him, so that from that time onwards the title of William Thomson's well-known work, *The Land and the Book,* would sufficiently describe his main line of studies.

After some weeks he wrote enthusiastically and hopefully to Père Larroca, Master-General of the Order, for more precise instructions; he then set out on a tour of Palestine and Transjordania that lasted several months. Since no instructions had reached him on his return, he left Palestine on July 15 to make an approach in person to his superiors. Thereafter, rival plans for his future were discussed, and it looked at one time as though he might be sent either to Fribourg in Switzerland as professor of New Testament exegesis or to his old house at Toulouse as professor of dogmatic theology. Then came a definitive order from the General sending him back to Jerusalem and his projected school, which was to have a house of philosophy and theology attached to it. On November 15, 1890, the École pratique d'études bibliques was opened by Père Lagrange in the presence of the French Consul-General and other friends of the School, who could hardly fail to notice that the rings to which the animals formerly sent to the slaughter house had been attached, were still visible on the walls of the *aula*. In his opening address the founder admitted that they were beginning "humbly, feebly, above all poorly, with a table, a blackboard, and a map as their whole teaching equipment." Père Vincent, one of the first arrivals in those early days, recalls the one table around which they all sat shoulder to shoulder, the one map that they soon knew by heart, and the one blackboard on which were written the various Semitic alphabets, nominal and verbal forms, paradigms, and the rest, which were transcribed and explained by Lagrange. He himself taught Hebrew, Assyrian, and Arabic, general introduction to Holy Scripture, and the history of the ancient East. He commented on various chapters of the historical books and was responsible for the management and organization of the School and the house of studies. He had, as his only resident assistant, another young Frenchman, Père Séjourné, who had charge of teaching the New Testament and the topography of Jerusalem and of conducting the weekly walks in and about the Holy City as well as the long journeys on horse- or camelback that were undertaken, two or three times yearly, through Palestine and the neighboring countries. A French secular priest of the Latin Patriarchate, the Abbé Heidet, who had been in Palestine since 1881, and had already journeyed many times through the land at a time when there was only one carriage road, gave help for more than a year with the teaching of the geography of the Holy Land. And, wonderful to relate, before the middle of the second year in the School's history, the École itself had been built and preparations had been made for the founding of the *Revue biblique*.

The launching of the *Revue* within two years or less of the School's opening has not, it seems to me, been discussed very fully either by Père Vincent in his obituary article on Père Lagrange in the *Revue biblique* for July, 1938, or by Père François Braun in his book on Lagrange's lifework mentioned earlier. The reasons for this relative silence are, no doubt, the same in both instances. In the first place, the earliest number of the *Revue*, dated as from December, 1891, has a good deal to say about the circumstances in which the periodical came to birth. In the second place, Lagrange himself has written in some detail about the matter in his little book, published in 1932, entitled *M. Loisy et le Modernisme*. Here he writes with much less than his usual reticence about "old, unhappy, far-off things, and battles long ago." Normally, it should be emphasized, he spoke little, if at all, about such matters. When he was attacked, he preferred to be silent. M. l'abbé Joseph Chaine, in his warm, charming, and appreciative study of the "Journée et Menus Propos du Père Lagrange" in the memorial volume, tells a story that well illustrates this aspect of Lagrange's character. It was in the month of July, 1930, when he had reached the age of seventy-five, that he was taking a walk with Abbé Vaganay, New Testament professor at Lyons, and, having recently been attacked in print, was on the point of discussing the matter with his companion. All of a sudden he stopped and exclaimed: "And yet I promised our Lord this morning during my meditation that I would not speak about this affair." And that was all he would say. In his reply to M. Loisy, written some two years after the incident just mentioned, he does, however, explain his position in the following terms:

A religious is accountable for his actions only to God, the Holy Father, and his superiors. If, however, he has written a good deal and if his actions have been judged to be baneful by pious folk animated by the best intentions, he will feel the need to explain his conduct to his brethren in the faith, and this is what I am doing here, because I cannot avoid speaking of the relations of M. Loisy with the *Revue biblique*. This most unwelcome task compels me to go back to a still earlier date, and even to touch upon personal matters. Here, then, I must interrupt the sequence of M. Loisy's *Mémoires* without, however, writing any other memoirs, unless it may be, in some part, the memoirs of the *Revue biblique*.[5]

He then gives, very briefly and in less than a page of large print, a résumé of his life-history before the founding of the School, stressing the point that: "I realized very well [at the time when he founded the School] that, having applied myself too late to the study of Oriental languages, I should never be a master in them. It was my endeavor, rather, to enlarge the field of my studies so that I might begin the training of those who, since then, have become my masters."

It was, he insists, not he, but the other resident professor of Scripture, Père Séjourné, who, having his full share of the faith that moves mountains, was determined that the School should have as its organ a review properly so styled. He himself had not, in those early days, even decided upon a bulletin to circulate among his fellow Dominicans that might contain news of expeditions and excursions, information about the subjects studied in the St. Stephen's curriculum, and details about pilgrimages to the Holy Places. The idea for such a bulletin which, at the present time, is in existence side-by-side with the *Revue biblique*, did not appeal to him. The far more ambitious scheme for a genuine review, to be printed in Paris and edited in Jerusalem, seemed to him quite fantastic. Père Séjourné, however, would give him no peace at all, and he was induced to take

[5]*M. Loisy et Modernisme*, p. 68.

counsel from two of the most eminent scholars in France, M. Vigouroux of the Paris theology faculty and M. Le Camus, later Bishop of La Rochelle from 1901 until his death in 1906. These men, like Séjourné, were in favor of a review properly so called, and they promised to contribute to it. Finally, quite shattered by this advice, Lagrange asked simultaneously for counsel and permission from Père Laboré, Vicar-General of the Dominican Order, who gave leave on condition that the initial subscriptions were sufficient to guarantee the *Revue* against any financial loss. This, writes Lagrange, was an amiable way of dismissing the matter *ad kalendas Graecas,* since subscribers are not easily found for a review not yet in existence. This remark is, perhaps, less well supported now than it would have been in the early nineties, but it must be remembered that the École suffered the additional disadvantage of being a new and as-yet-untried experiment. Nevertheless, a way of proceeding with the plan was at last discovered through the kind offices of Père Faucher, editor of a much appreciated text of the *Summa Theologica,* who had been a devoted friend of Père Matthieu Lecomte, founder of the original house in Jerusalem. Faucher was on good terms with the firm of Lethielleux in Paris, publishers of his edition of the *Summa,* and they agreed to bear all the expenses of the undertaking.

The next step, evidently, was to find contributors, and the first approach was made to Lagrange's dear masters of St. Sulpice, one of whom (Vigouroux) was hopeful of enlisting further support, whereas his disciple (Fillion), although sympathetic, preferred to remain in the background, and, so far as I am aware, never contributed any article or review, though in a much later work, *L'étude de la Bible,* he makes a gracious reference to the advantages of having studied at so renowned a school. The Society of Jesus contributed some illustrious names to the first list of writers for the *Revue,* though of the three first mentioned, Corluy, Cornely, and Knabenbauer, only the last named seems to have had an article in print—a Latin dissertation, "De peccato in Spiritu sanctum quod non remittatur," which appeared in the first (1892) volume. Among the Dominican contributors to the first numbers were the outstanding Assyriologist, Père Scheil, with Pères Faucher and Ollivier. Lagrange's friends in his Issy days, M. Batiffol and M. Hyvernat, also sent contributions, as did M. Thomas of Toulouse, M. Jacquier of Lyons, and M. Lesêtre of Paris. But, as Lagrange insists, no name among the first contributors attracted so much attention as did the absence of M. Loisy's name, since his two works on the canon of Scripture had already made his reputation as a scholar and a thinker. "His penetration, his critical temper, his clear and almost cutting manner of expressing his opinions, his extensive information, all made me desirous of gaining the collaboration of this force that could not but grow and increase."[6] There was, however, a lack of perfect unanimity about him in the minds of his contemporaries; some excellent authorities already thought his views were too advanced. It was not until about two years after the first number of the *Revue* appeared that Loisy's appointment as professor at the Institut Catholique de Paris was cancelled by the French hierarchy, and his contributions to the *Revue* (three in all) belong to the years 1895 and 1896. Only one of these was an article, the synoptic apocalypse being its subject; this piece, as Lagrange explains, ultimately proved an embarrassment both to the editorial board of the *Revue* and to M. Loisy himself.

The phrase "editorial board" just used is one that might easily be misunderstood. There was never any question of a double board, one in Paris and the other in Jerusalem. M. Vigouroux and M. Le Camus could and did bring the *Revue* to the notice of many readers who were entirely unknown to Lagrange and his Jerusalem colleagues, but they exercised no control over the articles published or the general tendency of the *Revue*. Lagrange did not wish his own name to appear on the title page, but the description given was clear. It was a quarterly biblical review, published under the direction of the professors at the school of biblical studies established in the Dominican House of St. Stephen, Jerusalem.

[6] *M. Loisy et Modernisme*, p. 71.

The first index to the *Revue,* which covers the volumes from 1892 through 1899, gives a list of all contributors to those eight volumes, and I have counted just over a hundred in all. The names and the titles of their publications occupy thirteen pages of rather small print, and out of this number two and one-half pages are taken up with Lagrange's varied writings during the eight formative years of the *Revue's* history. In all, I have reckoned that he contributed ninety-four items in the first eight years, and that these range from full-length articles of twenty and thirty pages to book reviews, short informative bulletins, accounts of journeys in the Holy Land and the surrounding countries, and summaries of the *acta* of sundry congresses of Orientalists. There were about thirty articles from his pen in the first eight years, some of them, as has been indicated, of considerable length.

Thus, in the year 1892, there were, in all, eight items written by Lagrange, beginning with an article on the topography of Jerusalem which proved that, from the start, topography and archaeology were both being studied along the right lines.Years later the most brilliant and original of all his disciples, the Dominican Père Louis Hugues Vincent, was to write in the volume of *Jérusalem Nouvelle,* which has as its chief subject matter the Church of the Holy Sepulchre, that, while it was a consolation to find that archaeology entirely supported the traditional claims, the inquiry into the facts had been carried out with rigid impartiality and according to the best available methods employed in the study of Greek or Roman antiquities.[7] In writing in this way he was merely continuing the tradition of the School from its earliest beginnings. In the first article in the *Revue,* Lagrange is at pains to demonstrate that the evidence was of such a kind that he was able, in Vincent's words, "to free himself from the chaos of incoherent systems and to fix the historical site of the primitive Jerusalem or City of David, and so to mark out the development of the Holy City in a way that later archaeological discoveries have confirmed at all points."[8]

What must strike every informed reader in those first numbers is not merely Lagrange's mastery and sureness of touch but his truly amazing versatility. Topography, geography, archaeological discoveries, traditions about the holy places, history and ethnography of the ancient East, Semitic or Greek epigraphy—all these, and many other subjects, seemed to be ever at his beck and call, so that the conditions laid down some forty years later by Professor Albright for the fruitful study of Israel and its history were already fulfilled in the still youthful founder of the Jerusalem School.[9] Lagrange bore little

[7]H. Vincent and F. M. Abel, *Jérusalem: Recherches de topographie, d'archéologie, et d'histoire* (Paris: Gabalda, 1914), II, p. 89.

[8]*RB,* XLVII (1938), p. 340.

[9]See the review of T. H. Robinson and W. O. E. Oesterley, *A History of Israel* in the *Journal of the Palestine Oriental Society,* XII, pp. 251-67.

resemblance to the type of learned men so amusingly castigated by Hilaire Belloc in his essay on "The Higher Criticism" whose "title 'Very Learned' (which gives them their authority) is tarnished by any form of general knowledge, and can only be acquired by confining oneself to a narrow field in which any fool could become an absolute master in about two years."

Something of Lagrange's wide aim and ample reach may be inferred from the titles of his other contributions to the *Revue* in that first adventurous year. There is a thirty-five page article on "The New History of Israel on the Prophet Hosea"; there are discussions of two inscriptions, one Phoenician and the other Palmyrene; there is a letter from Jerusalem detailing a visit to the River Jordan; there is an article on the Immanuel passage in Isaiah 7; and a note on pantheism in sacred history.

It will be of some interest for us to study the chief aims the young director of the School set before himself and his readers in the Foreword to the first number. The most important section of this introduction to the *Revue* and its function is that in which Lagrange justifies the need for a serious quarterly that will maintain a high standard and keep in touch with all that is best in biblical studies. He pleads for recognition of the fact that much of the scholarship displayed by Catholic France at the time of writing is derivative, and that in works to which he makes reference, the bibliographies contain twenty books in German or English to everyone in French. He

claims that the study of Hebrew in Catholic France is
not treated as something of real importance, yet "such
a study is indispensable for a thorough estimate even of
New Testament Greek." The proof of the inadequacy
of Hebrew studies in France is that there was, at that
time, no complete grammar and no Hebrew lexicon in
French, whereas Gesenius' grammar was then in its
twenty-fifth edition and his lexicon in its tenth. He com-
plains that France knows of no organized geographical
or topographical research in Bible lands, and contrasts
Victor Guérin on his solitary donkey with the excavations and mapwork carried out by English students of
the Bible. Again, he appeals to the fact that Hebrew is
not self-explanatory and that reference must be made to
the other Semitic languages. What, he asks, is the place
of each of these languages? Has the importance of Arabic
been somewhat exaggerated? In any event, there is
a virtually new language to be called in aid, namely As-
syro-Babylonian, considered by many to be, of all these
languages, the one most closely related to Hebrew, and
one that gives promise of an immense philological contribution to the study of the Hebrew Bible.

Lagrange is also insistent upon the enormous benefit
of working on the spot, which enables biblical students
to verify, often in a few days, topographical data or
disputed traditions.

Having in mind the fine library that was, in due
course, to be built up from gifts and countless "review

copies," he speaks of the need for bibliographies in books on Holy Scripture and clear references to the best available texts. He mentions, though not by name, the program of diocesan conferences in one of the French dioceses, which prints as a footnote the advice: "Consult the Talmud on this matter." But where, he asks, is the ordinary priest to find the Talmud? And even when he has found it, how is he to understand it?

Next, he faces, though only in passing, the question that has already been asked about the new *Revue*: Will its tendency be conservative or liberal? He decides that, when formulated in this manner, the question must remain unanswered since, properly speaking, these schools do not exist as distinct entities.

He ends his Foreword with the assurance that the *Revue biblique* will be directed, at one and the same time, in a Catholic spirit and in a scholarly spirit, but, as he informs us in his 1932 booklet, *M. Loisy et le Modernisme,* he felt that his own authority was quite insufficient in a matter of so much importance and that he must refer to one whose competence could not well be challenged—the renowned Dominican exegete from Spain, Cardinal Zeferino Gonzalez (1831-1894), whose work *La Biblia y la Ciencia* had been published in the preceding year, 1891. From him he takes a long quotation on the relative liberty of the Catholic biblical scholar. "In fact," wrote the Cardinal, "this amplitude in our criterion, this relative liberty in exegesis has never been so suitable, or even so necessary, as in our own days." This spirit of a conquistador, comments Lagrange, is not even yet fully appreciated by everybody. It was still less appreciated in 1892, and the Foreword, though examined in Rome and passed by censors, did not receive the approbation of the Master of the Sacred Palace, who did not wish in any way to take the responsibility for Cardinal Gonzalez and his ideas.

So the *Revue* was launched upon its long and distinguished career, and within a matter of months, Pope Leo XIII himself had given every possible encouragement to those who had been most helpful in the launching. Lagrange was then in Rome, without any expectation of receiving papal approval at so early a stage in the life of the publication, and there he met, for the first time, the Italian Dominican Cardinal, Tommaso Zigliara (1833-1893), in whose company he came to appreciate the extreme graciousness and distinction, coupled with every sign of intimacy, of a prince of the Holy Roman Church. Zigliara, who was a close friend of the Pope, offered his services to obtain not merely a formal blessing, but a definite sign of the Holy Father's interest and approval. Pope Leo's letter, dated the seventh of September, 1892, was printed in the *Revue* in the following year. It approved what seemed at the time to be a wholly original and special program (though, as Lagrange adds in parentheses, it was one that has been faithfully copied since then), namely, the exploration of the Holy Land by means of one-day excursions and expeditions lasting for several days or even weeks, lectures and conferences open to Catholics and non-Catholics alike, and publication of the *Revue*. His Holiness exhorted the members of the School to take heart afresh and to continue the good work, fortified in full measure by papal authority and good will.

Here it may be mentioned that, among Catholic reviews of a purely biblical character, the *Revue Biblique* appears to have been the forerunner of other periodicals now well known in the world of scholarship. Among these may be recorded the titles of *Biblische Studien* (1896), the *Biblische Zeitschrift* (1903), *Biblica* (1920), and *Verbum Domini* (1921). The *Catholic Biblical Quarterly* of America came into existence as recently as 1939, and the *Revista Biblica,* published in La Plata the same year. Later still came *Estudios Biblicos* (Madrid, 1929, with a new series in 1941-42), and *Cultura Biblica* (Segovia, 1944).

The point should, however, be made that most, if not all, of the later periodicals had their homes in some seat of learning where the articles and the other features would regularly be supplied by members of the faculty holding the offices of professor, lecturer, reader, *privat-docent*, and the like, ordinarily a fairly large body. Far different was the position at St. Stephen's, where in its early days there were only two resident members of the "biblical" staff, and some years had to elapse before the first students were able to make an effective contribution to the pages of the *Revue*. Holy Scripture, as we are all aware, is emphatically not a soft option. A friend of mine (the late Père Jacques Vosté, O.P., who died in 1949 in his tenth year as Secretary of the Pontifical Biblical Commission) always maintained that no teacher of the Bible could be said to know his subject until he had taught his course (in this instance a four-year cycle) three or four times. It is all the more remarkable that, within four or five years of their first entry into the School, some of the older students were already beginning to make their mark in their respective specialties. Père Louis Hugues Vincent's first article in the *Revue*, to which at the time of his death in 1960 he had been a contributor for sixty-four years, appeared in 1896 and was a description of the excavations carried out in Jerusalem between 1894 and 1897 by F. J. Bliss and A. C. Dickie. Père Antonin Jaussen, an expert in Arabic and author of standard works on Arab customs in the land of Moab and in the Nablus region, began his writing for the *Revue* a year later, in 1897, with a discussion of some Palmyrene inscriptions. Père Raphael Savignac's name does not occur at all before the year 1903, but from that time onwards until his death, nearly half a century later, he became a regular contributor, either alone or in association with Vincent or Jaussen. Edouard (in religion, Paul) Dhorme, who was born in 1881, and was a member of the School and of the

Dominican Order until 1931, and Felix-Marie Abel, his contemporary, were later arrivals and did not collaborate in the *Revue* until the years 1906 and 1903, respectively, but each of them has a long list of articles and reviews recorded in the Index for the years 1900 to 1908. There was a tradition at the time I studied under him that Dhorme had made a very early start as an Assyriologist, and had copied the cuneiform signs of the Code of Hammurabi not long after its first publication by Père Vincent Scheil, O.P., in the *Mémoires de la délégation en Perse*.[10] These are the great names among the older members of the School, but there were others who did useful work, and, as always, there were outside contributors, many of them former students at St. Stephen's.

It should be added that, with few exceptions, the articles and other features have been written in French. The distinguished Italian Orientalist, Professor Ignazio Guidi, in 1901 wrote the first article he sent to the *Revue* in his own language ("Il canone biblico della Chiesa copta"), and there were some articles in Latin by Hebrans, Knabenbauer, and Van Kasteren in the early numbers; but in the vast majority the contributions have been in French. This, as will be realized, has been at once a strength and a weakness, and has doubtless deprived the *Revue* of some articles that

[10]Vol. IV (1902), pp. 11 ff.

might have been submitted with profit to all concerned if it had not been for the existence of the
language barrier.

On one important point I have no reliable information at all; this concerns circulation of the periodical.
If any publicity has ever been given to this aspect of
its successful career, it has escaped me. I can only
surmise that, as the *Revue* has never lowered its high
standard by admitting the sort of article that largely
consists of other people's discoveries, its appeal has
been a somewhat restricted one throughout its history,
and the support given to it has usually been adequate
but scarcely sensational.

One of the many benefits conferred by the *Revue*,
as by all good periodicals, is that at all times it has
been a clearinghouse for ideas and a repository for
many articles that ultimately went into the making
of books. Between the year 1878 when he published
his thesis for the doctorate in law and the year 1894,
Lagrange produced no books. In 1894 there appeared
a work of some two hundred pages entitled *Saint-
Étienne et son sanctuaire à Jérusalem,* after which
there was a further hiatus until 1903, when the most
discussed of his earlier books, *La méthode historique,*
was published. But, in the meantime, as was to be
expected of a man of vast activity and energy, he was
preparing material for several future books in the
pages of the *Revue.* Sometimes, to be sure, the pro-

jected books never saw the light as separate entities, and this was true of his remarkable series on Genesis in the numbers for 1896 ("L'Hexaméron") and in 1897 ("L'innocence et le péché") and of two articles on biblical inspiration in 1896. It was not, in fact, until 1900 that his plan for a complete commentary on Holy Scripture, which foreshadowed the appearance of his many volumes in the "Études bibliques" series, was issued in the number for July, 1900. In this summary of the principles that were to govern the volumes in the series, Lagrange makes it clear that the texts to be translated and commented on will be the Hebrew, Aramaic, or Greek originals, and not that of the Latin Vulgate, and that a commentary cannot be expected to take the place of works by specialists in archaeology, geography, biblical history, or theology. Accordingly, volumes belonging to these specialties have appeared in the series side-by-side with commentaries properly so styled.

In 1901 the first of his articles on Semitic religions appeared, those dealing with the Semites in general and with the goddesses Asherah and Astarte. In the following year came a further article on the dead from the viewpoint of the Semitic religions, and in 1903 there appeared the earliest of the "Études bibliques" series. The first of these already mentioned for its fame, was the little treatise entitled *La méthode historique, surtout à propos de l'Ancien Testament.* It

prints the text of six lectures delivered to the church
students of the Institut Catholique de Toulouse, at
the request of the rector, Monsignor Pierre Batiffol.
The second (1904) edition was translated into English
by the Rev. Edward Myers, later, until his death in
1956, Archbishop-Coadjutor to Cardinal Griffin, Archbishop of Westminster, under the title, *Historical Criticism and the Old Testament.* The chief subjects
discussed in these lectures were biblical criticism and
the dogmas of the Catholic Church; doctrinal development in the Old Testament; the idea of inspiration
as it is found in the Bible; historical criticism and
natural science; the historical character of the Israelite
civil laws; and primitive history. From the start,
the book caused a good deal of disagreement and was
eventually followed by an *éclaircissement.* This last was
privately printed and never made available to the general
public. It is worth noting that *La méthode,* though disliked by many persons of importance, was never with-
drawn from circulation or made the object of any
ecclesiastical censure.

In the same year (1903) appeared the first commentary, properly so called, in the series: Lagrange's
Le Livre des Juges, a work of some four hundred
pages, which after more than sixty years is now not a
little out-of-date. There came also what is perhaps
the author's best work on an Old Testament subject,
the first edition of *Études sur les religions sémitiques,*

a book of 432 pages, to which a hundred pages more were added in the second (1905) edition. In a small pamphlet published in 1933 under the title *Semitic Religions* I wrote that: "This remains the only treatise on Semitic religions that approaches completeness, though it lays no claim to this quality" (p. 31). In the Foreword to the first edition Lagrange suggests that, if long titles were fashionable, the book would have been styled: "Certain studies on the Semitic religions in those matters that most closely affect the religion of Israel, either by reason of contrast in ideas or on account of resemblances in tradition and rites." Like Newman he was only too willing to choose titles that suggested a tentative or selective approach to his subject, and it is doubtless true that so much fresh evidence has now come to light that a mere revision of the book would not be of great value. In fact, even as long ago as 1923, Père Vincent told me that La-grange did not feel disposed to bring out a new edition, but that if he had attempted this, an almost complete rewriting would have been required. This does not alter the fact that these "Etudes" played a notable part in their time, and were described by Dr. Wilhelm Schmidt, author of *Der Ursprung der Gottesidee* and other works, as "the first dike set up against the evolutionary flood."

At about this time two matters were being con-sidered in Rome. One was the foundation of the

Pontifical Biblical Commission, which was effected
by Pope Leo XIII on October 30, 1902, through the
apostolic letter *Vigilantiae*. The other was the estab-
lishment of a Biblical Institute in Rome, and in this
Lagrange was, in Pope Leo's intention, to have a
notable part. The first list of consultors for the Commission appeared on November 30, 1902, and did not
include Lagrange's name. He was, however, appointed
to the office early in 1903, and the news was made
known to him by the General of the Order on January 26. In the following month he was summoned
to Rome and was told that the *Revue biblique*, while
remaining under his control and editorship, was to
become the official organ of the Commission in the
sense that it would publish any decrees, decisions, or
other matters which the cardinals and the consultors
had agreed to make public. He would also, as was
made clear to him, be attached to the Biblical Institute which the Pope already had in mind. In April
of 1903 he sought leave to return to Jerusalem, at
least for a time, and the Pope willingly gave permission, promising, however, that he would later be recalled to Rome and be given work to do "auprès de
Nous." The Pope's death on July 20 of that year
put an end to these projects, though for some years
after 1903 the *Revue* was privileged to print the Commission's decrees as they were issued.

Something has been said about the first works to appear in the "Études bibliques" series and it should be added that the volumes have continued to appear at intervals, even though the original plan for a complete commentary on the Bible is still far from being realized. Yet, a series that includes such major works as the commentaries on Isaiah and Jeremiah by the Jesuit Father Albert Condamin, Canon van Hoonacker's *Minor Prophets,* Dhorme's *Job,* Abel's *Maccabees,* and Podechard's *Ecclesiastes* may well be considered to have earned a leading position in the world of biblical learning. Among works in the series that are not commentaries a special place must be given to Père Vincent's *Canaan d'après l'exploration récente,* published in 1906, when the author was not quite thirty-five. Of the various chapters on such topics as Canaanite cities, cultic centers, idols, the dead, and Canaanite pottery, perhaps the most generally interesting is the very able and informed sketch of Canaan in general history. Since this book was written, the great change referred to by Professor Albright in his essay "The Old Testament and the Archaeology of Palestine" in the symposium on *The Old Testament and Modern Thought* (1951) has come about, but in his Penguin volume, *The Archaeology of Palestine,* Albright pays a fine tribute to Vincent's work and example, and hails him as "facile princeps" in these studies.

It is unnecessary to say much about Vincent's later work, which includes his book *Jérusalem*, prepared in collaboration with Abel, and his later volumes on *Jérusalem de l'Ancien Testament*.

These are some of the works that have been carried out, in part or as a whole, and the *Revue biblique* itself has survived two world wars, though during the German occupation of France it had to change its title to the symbolic and appropriate one of *Vivre et Penser*. It continues to flourish under the inspiring editorship of Père Pierre Benoit, present director of the School, who resembles the founder in two ways in particular—in his profound and many-sided learning, and in his almost excessive modesty and simplicity.

Lagrange himself survived into extreme old age and died on March 10, 1938, three days after his eighty-third birthday. It has not been necessary to say a great deal about his personal history, because, as Vincent insists, from the time of the first foundations his life was that of the School. The chief, but not the only, interruption was early in the First World War, when he and some of his students were made prisoners by the Turks and were destined for a concentration camp at Urfa. From this prospect they were delivered en route through the intervention of Pope Benedict XV. Lagrange was working in France again early in 1915 and, in his own amazing way,

was able to keep the *Revue* going during the war
years and, in addition, to write his commentaries on
Romans and Galatians, his minor masterpiece, *Le sens
du Christianisme d'après l'exégèse allemande,* a volume
entitled *Mélanges d'histoire religieuse,* and, of course,
various articles in periodicals other than the *Revue
biblique.* The School was reopened in 1919. Almost
the only student not a Dominican was the late Abbé
Chaine, who had the room opposite mine at the Pro-
cure de St. Sulpice during the scholastic year 1920
to 1921. Towards the end of his life the climate of
Palestine proved too severe for Lagrange, and he was
ordered by his doctors to seek habitation in a more
temperate zone. He chose to return to his Dominican
house, where he had spent his novitiate many years
before, St. Maximin, near Marseilles. There, in the
first days of October, 1937, I visited him and was
privileged to hear his always fresh and original views
on a number of topics, and to admire his continuing
vigor of mind which had led him to take up again his
commentary on Genesis, laid aside for more than thirty
years. Both sight and hearing were affected, but he
continued to lecture to the students and to take his
full share in the life of the community. He was still
engaged in teaching and writing in the first days of
the following March. He lectured for the last time
on March 4, on the Passion of our Lord as related in
the Synoptists and St. John, and on the eighth the

pen fell from his hand at the end of an article, the last of so many to be printed in the *Revue biblique,* on the Mosaic authenticity of Genesis and the documentary hypothesis. With the half-finished word "Jerusalem" on his lips he passed to the fuller life on March 10, 1938.

There are many things that might be said of him, but I must confine myself to two or three. First, he was, above all, a cheerful and encouraging teacher, who could get the best out of his material and was always willing to discuss a question without any air of authority or special learning. He had a very tender heart and could easily be hurt, but he disliked any suspicion of a *cher maitre* attitude on the part of his students, which was indeed quite foreign to his nature.

Again, he would have been the last person to dragoon his students on the lines of the bellman in *The Hunting of the Snark*: "What I tell you three times is true." When he saw a student taking notes of his lecture without due attention to the text, he bounded from his seat, rushed over to the man's desk, and pointed to the words of Holy Scripture, crying: "Look for yourself and please *don't* take my word for it! It was not for nothing that, when I founded the School, I called it a *practical* school of biblical studies!"

He was, moreover, a thoroughly honest scholar who in his lectures intensely disliked talking about any subject of which he had no first-hand knowledge.

Monsignor de Solages, now rector of the Catholic faculty of Toulouse, gives an example of this in the *Mémorial Lagrange*. A student had asked the Father one day about the critical value and importance of the Armenian versions of the Gospels. "I dislike speaking of what I do not know," was his reply, "and I do not know Armenian." Then he added: "However, if you are really interested, I will tell you the opinion commonly held by specialists in Armenian." And then followed a quite admirable and learned account of the position. Monsignor de Solages comments that more than one of Lagrange's hearers thought in his heart that this was a very curious way of not knowing, but the whole incident was quite characteristic of the man.

He was always on his guard against any unnecessary interruption of his working hours, particularly those precious hours of the morning, from seven o'clock onwards, when he had returned to his cell after his scanty *petit déjeuner*. He normally rose at five, offered Holy Mass, made a long thanksgiving, and swept out his cell before going down to breakfast. He then had the joyful prospect of nearly five hours of close study ahead of him. L'abbé Chaine gives an amusing account of his own well-meant efforts to wish Lagrange a happy new year early on the morning of January 1, 1920. As he entered the Father's cell those kind but very penetrating eyes looked at him from behind the great deal table at which Lagrange did his work. "What do you want?" he asked. "Mon

Père," stammered poor Chaine, himself one of the kindest and most considerate of men, "I came to wish you a happy new year!" "We shall exchange our good wishes this afternoon," was the answer. "This is not the time for it. Now I am working!" And before his visitor had a chance to turn right about, Lagrange was once more bent over his books. It seemed, and was, a hard discipline for one who loved good talk and pleasant company, but it was a small price to pay for the immense collection of books and articles that represent his contribution to scholarship.

In even higher matters than scholarship it could be said of him, as of Cardinal Newman that: "His was a life of prayer." His spiritual testament may be quoted as some proof of this.

> I declare before God that it is my intention to die in the Holy Catholic Church to which I have always belonged with my whole heart and soul since the day of my baptism, and to die faithful to my vows of poverty, chastity, and obedience in the Order of St. Dominic. To that end I commend myself to my good savior Jesus, and to the prayers of his most holy Mother, who has always been so good to me.
> I declare also most explicitly that I submit to the judgment of the Apostolic See all that I have written. I believe that I can add that I have always had the intention in all my studies of contributing to what is good— I mean to the reign of Jesus Christ, the honor of the Church, and the benefit of souls. And I wish above all to add that I am a son of Mary. *Tuus sum ego, salvum me fac.*

2: HISTORY IN THE BIBLE Father Albert Marie-Joseph Lagrange, of the Friars Preachers, represented in his own person the coming of age of biblical scholarship in the Catholic Church in this century. He lived through a period of stress which has its lessons for our own day, as I hope to suggest here. He enriched all who love the Bible with that variety of important gifts which will be recalled over and over again in these papers: namely, the *Revue biblique,* an outstanding journal in these matters through all of its seventy-two volumes up to 1966; the "Études bibliques," solid and enduring works of commentary and of synthesis; and the École biblique et archéologique française, the research institute and graduate school in Jerusalem, which sets a standard for international scholarship in its field. That heritage has grown and flourished in the twenty-eight years since Père Lagrange was called to his reward. I will mention only that the one-volume *Bible de Jérusalem,* which is in some ways the distillation of all the various projects that have Father Lagrange for their founder, is undoubtedly the most effective single source in Christendom for attaining to the full measure of what the Holy Spirit has stored up for us in the Sacred Books. But with all that, the gift that means most to many of us today is the example of his life.

I will try to put that in terms of "Père Lagrange and History in the Bible," because that history is a current topic among us; and it is a way, I think, in which the example can be understood. Father Maly's topic is Père Lagrange and the Pentateuch; you will excuse me, therefore, if I go to the other end, in a sense, of Old Testament history, and take my example from the Book of Judith, with which I have lately been concerned. For those who may not share the Catholic conviction that the Book is inspired, the choice will perhaps seem somewhat strange; but if they will bear with me, I think they will at least see that we understand our own problems and face them in their proper terms.

It was in 1890 that Father Lagrange, for some years ordained a Dominican priest, having intensive language training at the University of Vienna behind him, left for Jerusalem to begin the long lifetime of mature scholarship for which we honor him now. A few months earlier, an old friend of his from seminary days at Issy, near Paris, had come to America on a similar errand as the first professor engaged for the new Catholic University in Washington. And so it happens that there sits on the shelves of the library where I work in Washington an edition, the earliest, of the *Dictionnaire apologétique de la Foi Catholique*, published in 1889.

It has an article on Judith, which details the usual complex of arguments for seeking in that book a demonstrable historicity in the details of the narrative, makes Luther the adversary, and ends up by dating the events of Judith in the days of the captivity of Manasseh, king of Judah, in the mid-seventh century before Christ. It gives a cross-reference to an article under that king's name, which discusses some of the seventh-century Assyrian records as they were then known, and ends up by saying, "Thus does true science defend true religion." Now it was true religion, all right; but it has proved to be extremely limited science. Father Lagrange saw this quite early as a danger, and reflecting on the approach which it embodies, he said: "A perpetual defense of the Bible does not do justice to its dignity." He means, of course, that the defense alone is not enough; and that in deriving — as we are bound to do — the lessons taught through the human author of a sacred book, we cannot afford to impose on that author purposes and interests which are ours, not his, and which have nothing to do with his place and time and theme. What one defends in such a case is no longer the dignity or the inerrancy of Holy Writ.

About the turn of the century, the study of the Book of Judith among Catholics went through a phase of

what was called "history according to appearances."
A number of Catholic writers adopted views that saw
in certains books of the Old Testament (usually To-
bit, Judith, and Esther) narratives that were not intended to convey strict history, but something in the
nature of a parable or an allegory, in which a moral
exhortation, or the like, was enveloped in a seemingly
historical framework.

What made this kind of explanation attractive, however, were not considerations of literary or historical
criticism such as would have some intimate relation
to the nature of the book under discussion. Rather,
it was the ease with which certain problems regarding
the language of the Old Testament could be resolved
once it was recognized that the sacred writers normally had no intention of conveying about matters of
astronomy or other natural sciences any more than
the usual popular impressions by which we govern
our daily speech: for example, we say the sun rises,
though it is the earth that moves. There is, then, in
the Bible a kind of "science according to appearances." Why not, some said, "history according to
appearances" along similar lines? The phrase became
so popular that even Father Lagrange actually used
it. He was careful to point out from the beginning,
however, that in the nature of things the sacred writer's interest in history could never be simply equated
with his presumed indifference toward the niceties of

physical science. And in the last of his conferences on the "Méthode historique," delivered in 1902, Father Lagrange specified that the proper approach to understanding how far a biblical writer commits himself to a presentation of historicity in detail, is through a related understanding of the nature of the *genre* or literary form he has chosen to employ. And would you believe it: of the few extraordinary minds among Catholics in our day who will accept no testimony on the importance of literary forms for the appreciation of the biblical books as a whole, either from Father Lagrange or from Pope Pius XII, it is still possible to find one who will go back sixty years to "history according to appearances," as though the state of the question were somewhere there.

By 1903, however, neither literary forms nor historical criticism were exactly popular in Catholic theological circles. There could be many reasons for this: but the reason that grew and persisted was basically fear—fear of that insidious surge of apostasy from the faith on specious intellectual grounds now known as Modernism. Father Lagrange had met its challenge head on and forthrightly as soon as it became clear that supposedly Catholic writers were in fact undermining the foundations of the faith. Now, when one is afraid of a plague, it is hardly a prudent manifestation of that fear to clamor for the quarantine of a qualified public health doctor who is currently engaged in checking its inroads: and yet in the case of Father Lagrange, that is approximately what happened. So violent was the storm that in the end it meant a new orientation of his work. He had a commentary on Genesis ready to publish in 1906; but he was persuaded by higher authority within the Church to desist from it, and later was requested to turn his attention to New Testament and related topics instead. Those who are not Catholic always find it hard to understand how this can be. One remarkable answer to that lies in the results, when the servant of the Church is of the stature of a Father Lagrange. The work he did in the New Testament field made him easily the most distinguished exegete of those sacred books in the Church of his generation: to claim no more. And whatever the needs in the Old Testament field may have been, the absence of his Gospel studies would have left an unquestionably greater void! A not dissimilar case at my own university gave the Netherlands its most distinguished Catholic champion of social action.

For those who are Catholic, the lesson, I think, lies elsewhere. Official endorsement within the Church of new approaches to the truth that are good and useful comes slowly at times: but it comes. Father Lagrange himself saw only the dawn in his last year among us. He took up again for publication the materials on Genesis that he had laid aside in 1906. He was correcting the proofs when he died. When the study appeared in the *Revue biblique* for 1938, for the first time in all the serried volumes filled with his writings, one got the impression of not looking forward, but back over the journey traversed. The new discoveries are faithfully recorded and carefully weighed, but the glance is backward just the same. Small wonder, since the basic text had lain in his trunk for thirty years!

Let us go back to the Book of Judith. If Father Lagrange's major scholarly works were in other directions, his views on Old Testament questions transpired quite clearly from the thoughtful and incisive reviews that appeared from his pen in the *Revue biblique*. There was one such in 1908, when he congratulated a Catholic writer on the strength of the case he had made out for the origin of the Book of Judith in Maccabean times. Since, however, the same writer had also developed the notion that the specific events and persons contained in the Book had reference to four different periods, and went back to four sources more or less contemporary with the several sets of facts, Père Lagrange went on to say:

> And then, when a Book that deals with historical times is so far outside the conditions of history that no one has been able to reconstitute the facts and put them in harmony with history as such; since the personal names and the place names cannot be reconciled; since nobody can propose a plausible solution without chang-

ing these names, and without altering the physiognomy of the text in consequence, is it not more respectful to the Holy Spirit who has inspired this Book, to take it as it is, and to draw out of it the religious lesson which it bears, rather than to create for it a history in spite of itself, or four histories, in spite of a certain unity in the composition?

He also comments, dryly, that the advantage of an appeal to the Persian period for Judith is that it yields room for the long interval of peace spoken of in the Book, allowing Judith to attain the age of 105 years, without having to join those authors who make her seventy years of age when she captivated Holofernes.

A more varied review appeared in the same quarterly in 1916. It had to do with parts of a new edition of the *Dictionnaire apologétique de la Foi Catholique,* then in course of publication. First there is reference to an entry on Job, whose author had struggled to underscore his conviction that a historical substratum for the poem really existed. Père Lagrange observed: "The apologetic for our faith would perhaps be more solid if we were to insist on the splendid light of biblical teaching in the midst of the darkness of ancient religious thought, rather than cling doggedly to points one does not even dare to propose as being certain." Next, there is question of Jonah. To quote Father Lagrange:

The history of Jonah is known, and even more than the text of that history, the difficulties to which it has given rise. Père Condamin sets them forth, and balances against them the answers of the so-styled traditional exegesis. But besides these "answers" painfully erected on the basis of sailors' yarns too often false to begin with, there exists another solution. It is what the author calls the "hypothesis of didactic writing." He was noticeably satisfied to base himself on the authority of M. van Hoonacker in his quite distinguished commentary on the Twelve Minor Prophets. [This had appeared shortly before in the "Études bibliques" series.]

Father Condamin is then quoted with approval for having said:

One must not without strong reasons abandon an interpretation that is common in the Catholic Church. But one can reflect that in past centuries the historical and literary questions relative to the Sacred Books had not been studied as they are in our day. Thus one had not the same difficulties, the same problems to solve.

Then comes the part that has to do with Judith. The author of the article, again Père Albert Condamin, S.J., had taken a stand for the substantial historicity of the Book, but said that historicity in detail was something else again. Father Lagrange gave a summary of his views, and then objected that the accumulation of points which Père Condamin did not take to be historical as presented, was no longer a matter of details. Father Lagrange added:

History written in this manner is no longer history. It would be less contrary to a sound doctrine of inspiration to admit that a sacred writer freely set forth conventional figures to teach what he had at heart, than to imagine that he had in mind to compose history by bedecking a true historical nucleus with traits accumulated haphazard from histories foreign to his theme. Besides, P. Condamin concludes his apologetic treatment of the Book by saying, "If truly solid proofs demonstrating the fictional character of the whole story were to be adduced, this would in no respect compromise the inspiration of the Book; it would belong to a different literary genre, that is all: it would be a parable, a parenetic fiction, an edifying story."

Let us ask now the question, keeping ourselves to the Old Testament for the moment, what precisely is new about current Catholic exegesis of a Book like Job, or Jonah or Judith, as one might find it in the *Bible de Jérusalem*, or in a Paulist pamphlet? Mainly, one thing is new: namely, that in 1943 Pope Pius XII, in his encyclical *Divino afflante Spiritu*, in full awareness of the currents of thought I have been suggesting to you, obliged the exegetes of the entire Catholic world to the diligent use of the methodology and the tools which Père Lagrange and his associates in Jerusalem had been employing since 1890; the Pope said it was an inescapable part of their sacred duty. Specifically, respecting problems having to do with the inerrancy of Holy Scripture, Pope Pius urged the Catholic commentator to "determine to what extent the manner of expression or the literary mode adopted by the sacred writer may lead to a correct and genuine interpretation; and let him be convinced that this part of his office cannot be neglected without serious detriment to Catholic exegesis." That does not mean, of course, that literary criticism becomes in any sense the goal of biblical studies; or that Catholic scholars will not at times fall short of complete success in their conscientious efforts to use these tools—the more so as not everyone, obviously, became a Père Lagrange in 1943, or since.

I think, however, that I can make this claim: namely, that in the twenty-odd years since the publication of the *Divino afflante Spiritu,* Catholic exegesis of the Old Testament has reached a point where one of Father Lagrange's visions from his earliest days has been in essence fulfilled, in that there remains no difficulty, from the historical side, touching the inerrancy of any portion of the Old Testament message, to which the Catholic exegete is without the elements for a solution. Sometimes, in fact, in our study of the biblical narratives, history regains its own in rather extraordinary ways. If I may inject a personal note, I think I have been able to demonstrate lately that the Book of Judith is a meditation on an earlier biblical text, namely, Exodus 14:31; that its proper function is that of an inspirational story for Passover; and that the history on which it very clearly bases the whole tenor of its narrative is the actual intervention of God in behalf of his people at the crossing of the Reed Sea, and again at the deliverance of Jerusalem as portrayed in Isaiah and in certain Psalms. That the Almighty will continue this historic work of salvation insofar as the dispositions of his people prepare them for that providential action, is the message of the Book. It is a message of hope; and we all know that the New Testament fulfillment is in transcendent terms, not available to the Old Testament writer.

Looking back over the interests of Père Lagrange having to do with historical studies and their relation to the Bible, as reflected especially in his "Méthode historique," I wonder if one other of the problems he set himself has not become much more urgent in our day than it was in his, though he saw it clearly enough. It is not a problem that has to do with the touchy matter of the inerrancy of Scripture, particularly. Rather it is an apologetic question that calls for an answer, with an eye to the world of men outside the Christian faith. I think of that problem in connection with a casual visit to Père de Vaux, successor, then, to Father Lagrange as director of the École biblique. It was in early March, I think, of 1956. Some visitors from America wanted to see where the well-known scrolls had been found, so down we went by the Jericho road to the edge of the Dead Sea, and there were the archaeologists' tents. Not where I had expected, however. It seems the Bedouin had found a new cave, and there had been manuscripts in that one, too. I do not think we were unwelcome visitors, but we interrupted a strange and thankless task. The cave was about forty feet deep into the cliffs, and a rock fall centuries ago had made it practically inaccessible except to thousands of generations, I suppose, of thousands of bats. These bats were of interest to the Bedouin, because the deposit of guano which they had built up on the floor of the cave, several feet thick in places, could be sold for money. So they had pried their way into the cave, to the indignation of the bats, and they found not only the guano, but some rope, and pots, and leather manuscript scrolls from the Roman period. What Father de Vaux was doing, however, was an unasked-for consequence of all of that. When he and his technicians and laborers had done with the guano and the remains of the Roman period, they then found themselves with evidence of an earlier occupation of the cave, from the Chalcolithic period, about 3500 years before Christ. Now the good citizens of the Chalcolithic had not yet developed the art of writing so as to leave manuscripts among the crumbly fragments of their pottery jars, but a conscientious archaeologist cannot afford to neglect them, all the same. So there was Father de Vaux, gleaning from that unpleasant cave the meager remains of an occupation level that was easily 1500 years forgotten when Abraham came to Palestine.

The point is that, in our generation, time and God's timing are, in relation to the human race, if not a theological, at least an apologetic problem. Already

Father Lagrange felt bound to make the point that the Old Testament is not, nor is it intended to be, a thumbnail sketch of the history and prehistory of the human race. Abraham is a very junior citizen of the world indeed, and those who are without our faith are inclined to display a certain smugness about that fact, almost as though they thought they knew something of which we were not aware. In the fullness of time, our Lord came; and a proper part of the duty of every Old Testament scholar is to trace in sacred history the development of the readiness to be aware of Christ when he would come, and to accept God's saving purposes through his Son. But what of the older, the providential development not so overtly supernatural, as we look at it, whereby the Almighty prepared the whole human race, all of whom he wishes to save and to bring to a knowledge of the truth, for the initial fact of Abraham, one man of faith; and then for the facts of Moses, and the Prophets, and Christ? The two developments are part of one divine plan, and it would seem that in our day it is incumbent upon biblical scholars, because they are in closer contact with the data, to indicate to their more abstrusely theological brothers as best they can the general lines of the process by which God steadily led, as he surely did, stone age, Chalcolithic, and ancient pagan man to the capability of measuring up, in some degree, to the social fact which is the Christian Church.

Père Braun, in discussing the impression made on Père Lagrange by Palestine in the first year of his work there, notes that he found it a living commentary on the Bible. That it surely is, for the Old Testament as well as for the New. From our increasing understanding and need for understanding of God's way with men, we see also, today, that with the shaping of the more lowly aspects of man's physical and social control of his environment, the way was prepared for a social partnership of all men in the supreme mystery of Christ and his Mystical Body. Are there not, therefore, providential elements also in the curious fact that the Holy Land is the place on earth best suited to be a kind of laboratory for the study of human life continuously, with no major periods missing, from the most remote antiquity through all stages of social and community development, right on into historical times and identifiably supernatural fact of Abraham?

I believe that there are, and that the task of Père de Vaux which I described so blithely has a convergent value for the purposes for which Père Lagrange went to Palestine in the first place. Similarly, it does not seem to me that the interest of the Old Testament scholar or of the Christian apologist in the remains of ancient Jericho dating back to the Mesolithic period, some eight or nine thousand years before Christ, can be limited to establishing that the evidence for the days of Joshua has been eroded away from the top of the mound. There is something to be put into a religious perspective in all this, and it is related to the salvation, in our day, of those whom the Gospel has not yet reached—which is the problem rather in terms of space, that I have been suggesting in terms of time.

Therefore, it seems to me that there is an ultimate religious value which we cannot yet measure, but which has Providence behind it, in the fact that Père Lagrange established upon Palestinian soil an institute whose members not only contribute copiously and richly to the understanding of that abiding work of the Holy Spirit which is the Bible, but also have the courage and the perseverance to raise up out of the dust and to interpret for what there is in them, even the meager traces of ancient man, through whom also God was working out the one, eternal plan.

Returning, now, to questions that have to do with the Bible and the identifiably supernatural, there is no denying the fact that studies carried out from a perspective that puts literary and historico-critical considerations in the foreground can, usually in the hands of popularizers, result in oversimplification, exaggeration, or neglect of more profound matters. In recent years there have been two expressions of concern from the Holy See that this has, in certain quarters, been so. I will mention, only, the restrained and careful warning of the Holy Office, of June 20, 1961, which should be in the minds of all of us, and on which it would be presumptuous of me to comment. (Some others seemingly have no hesitation in reading into it at will things that are not there at all, such as that by and large professional exegetes have been seriously derelict in their duty.) The other expression of concern is in the encyclical *Humani generis* of 1950, which attends, among many other things, to a heedless tendency to equate certain Old Testament narratives with myths. In dealing with this problem, however, the Holy Father makes his own two expressions we might well dwell upon. He says of the first eleven chapters of Genesis (quoting a letter of the Pontifical Biblical Commission to Cardinal Suhard of Paris) that "in simple and metaphorical language adapted to the mentality of a people of lowly culture, they both state the principal truths which are fundamental for our salvation, and also give a popular description of the origin of the human race and of the chosen people." In that quotation, the word "metaphorical" connotes a literary judgment; the Holy Father uses it, and he applies it to the entire eleven chapters, without deeming it necessary to make distinctions. Similarly, in dealing with the truly delicate question of how these same chapters of Genesis relate to history, the Pope again makes his own the language of the letter to Cardinal Suhard, which, he says, "clearly points out that . . . although properly speaking not conforming to the historical method used by the best Greek and Latin writers or by competent authors of our time, [these chapters] do nevertheless pertain to history in a true sense, which however must be further studied and determined by exegetes." By whom? By exegetes. This, therefore, is a reiteration of the mind of the same Supreme Pontiff—made clear in the *Divino afflante Spiritu*—that the biblical exegete has a function and a responsibility to perform in matters of importance to the Church. Without doubt, it is to be performed in the spirit of a Father Lagrange, so that in all cases the pertinent theological considerations and the analogy of the faith shed all their light on the judgment to be formulated; and that judgment has to be subject always to the sovereign right of Holy Mother Church to witness definitively to what is in fact concordant with the teaching she has received from Christ.

Yet, the vote of confidence is there, even with the warning. It is the same pontifical voice which had said some years before: "There remain therefore many things, and of the greatest importance, in the discussion and exposition of which the skill and genius of Catholic commentators may and ought to be freely exercised, so that each may contribute his part to the advantage of all, to the continued progress of sacred doctrine and to the defense and honor of the Church." Now let us ask ourselves what merited this vote of confidence by Pope Pius XII, re-echoed in fact in the last year of his pontificate in a communication to the Catholic Congress for Biblical Studies at Brussels in 1958? The clue is in the *Divino afflante,* in the passage which says:

Thus it has come about that confidence in the authority and historical value of the Bible, somewhat shaken in the case of some by so many attacks, today among Catholics is completely restored; . . . *[and, after a reference to opinion outside the Church, he continues:]* This change is due in great part to the untiring labor by which Catholic commentators of the Sacred Literature, in no way deterred by difficulties and obstacles of all kinds, strove with all their strength to make suitable use of what learned men of the present day, by their investigations in the domain of archaeology or history or philology, have made available for the solution of new questions.

Many no doubt have their place in that encomium by the Holy Father; but in 1943 it would have been impossible as it is now, to find another to whom the words apply in the same measure as to Father Lagrange. The historical sense of the Pope's words, which refer to the period from Leo XIII to his own day, resides in that prudent, conscientious devotion to the cause of truth of which, in the generation in question, Père Lagrange was the standard bearer and the model.

The lesson, I would say, has not been lost on the Catholic exegetes of today. At this point, I wish to do two things: I wish to restrict myself, as I have not done before, to Catholic biblical scholarship in the United States and Canada; and I wish to extend my remarks, as I have not done before, to include my New Testament colleagues in what I have to say. Father Lagrange carried out his magnificent undertaking in a generation filled with apprehension; he was called a

Modernist, against justice, and charity, and common sense. There are no Modernists today in the United States and Canada among biblical scholars in the Catholic Church. To this statement I will add only that it would take two generations of cultivated ignorance, combined with a singular lack of charity for one's fellow priests, compounded by an inexcusable unawareness of their persons and their work, to enable anyone to suggest that there are. Less serious but equally surprising is the fact that some, brought up—as I was myself—in a genuine vacuum with regard to biblical study, a situation which Pope Pius XII in the *Divino afflante Spiritu* specifically set out to remedy, feel nonetheless free to draw up a long catalogue of the supposed liberties and errors of biblical exegetes in dealing with the sacred text. They do so without any attempt to accept or to come to grips with the principles and methods laid down by the Holy Father as important for the settling of the points at issue—principles and methods in many cases given to the modern Church by Father Lagrange. And our poor friends have yet to learn that the rest of the Catholic Church has joined him in putting those principles and methods into operation! It becomes a little comical when, in the name of nineteenth-century secular historicism, the same man blandly expects that you will find for him Bethomastem in the hill country of Samaria, or Phud and Lud, for that matter, side-by-side in continental Asia, to gratify his strange notion of how the Holy Spirit should have employed his free human instrument; and then in the next breath has the gall to complain that biblical scholars are so busy with the minutiae that the light and warmth of the biblical message are not transmitted in their commentaries.

I am suggesting, as you see, that there are lessons for our day to be learned from the life of Father Lagrange by others than biblical exegetes. I have tried to indicate that in Old Testament matters, there has been attained among Catholic scholars a plateau of relative tranquillity and accord; and that there is no reason to suppose that the fruits of this will confer anything but increasing benefits on Catholic life. Is it then so surprising that in our day the most widely agitated problems related to history should be in the field of New Testament studies? It is not in the nature of any study, even on the most sacred subjects, to be without problems. In his own Order, and in the house which he founded, Père Lagrange has today worthy successors in the work of New Testament scholarship to which he devoted so much of his life. I refer of course to Père Boismard, and above all to Père Benoit. Their work is serious work; it is conducted with the prudence, the fortitude, and the inner tranquillity that marked the career of Père Lagrange. Its results are widely accessible in the pages of the *Bible de Jérusalem*. And the Church in France, which has known Modernism, and has known Père Lagrange, is not being disturbed by bogymen.

There are other parts of the Catholic world, and I will not be invidious by naming any but our own, where the generation represented by Père Lagrange left a notable gap in Catholic scholarship in the biblical field. Make what exceptions and allowances you may choose out of piety to make: the fact is still there. It is true that present-day New Testament studies within the Church show some developments that were perhaps not foreseen by Père Lagrange, or even by Pope Pius XII. It is true also that certain aspects of Gospel study are involved with highly complex interrelationships that pose difficult problems for literary and historical criticism, and tend, incidentally, to spark the impatience of those who would presume to simple and immediate answers. In these circumstances everybody has some experience of stress, and it cannot be denied that the repercussions of this have been felt at the Ecumenical Council of the Church, with consequences happy for biblical studies thus far. Our New Testament scholars have indeed need of prudence, as who does not; but it will cease to be a virtue if it is not accompanied by fortitude in the spirit of Father Lagrange—which may God grant them, for the Church in the United States could ill afford at this point any slackening in the present flourishing growth of its biblical scholarship.

One thing Pope Pius XII most surely did foresee— helped in so doing, quite certainly once again, by the remembered struggles of Père Lagrange. We who work one way or another in the biblical field like to quote the passage, not merely, as some might think, because it gives us some earnest of a support that is indispensable and precious in matters important to us; but also because it is the reminder of victory won, against odds such as do not exist today.

> Let all the other sons of the Church bear in mind that the efforts of these resolute laborers in the vineyard of the Lord should be judged not only with equity and justice, but also with the greatest charity; all moreover should abhor that intemperate zeal which imagines that whatever is new should for that very reason be opposed or suspected.

There follows shortly the passage I quoted to you earlier, to the effect that there remain many important tasks for the Catholic commentator in the advancement of Catholic doctrine and the defense and honor of the Church. I have said that Father Lagrange won a struggle against odds. Indeed, it shows a fine discernment of the nature of the changing times on the part of Pope Pius, that in 1943 he saw no need to set standards for biblical exegetes with respect to the dispositions they should have toward one another among their own kind. As for more recent times, in the past couple of years I have seen in print, issuing from the most unexpected sources, testimonials to the *esprit de corps* among Catholic students of the Bible. It is sometimes even suggested, by the same indignant witnesses, that we manage to emulate Father Lagrange in yet another of his more notable qualities: we get along pretty well with scholars who are not even Catholic.

And now, perhaps, a final reflection on the times in which we are. In what terms Pope John XXIII is going to be characterized by his grateful sons and daughters in the days to come, one should not claim to know. We did see in him an all-embracing charity; and for those within the Church, a desire on his part for that liberty which is the condition for true harmony of spirit, and for the flowering of charity itself. The Vatican Council may be expected, in God's providence, to reflect those qualities of him who convened it; and we look forward to biblical studies, among the multiple, worldwide activities of the Church, being bathed in that sunlight. But when, please God, they are, there will be other figures in this century whom those concerned with biblical matters will not forget: Pope Pius XII, who put the example into words, and gave it his authority: "This true liberty of the children of God, which adheres faithfully to the teaching of the Church and accepts and uses gratefully the contributions of profane science, this liberty, upheld and sustained in every way by the confidence of all, is the condition and source of all lasting fruit and of all solid progress in Catholic doctrine"; and Père Lagrange, the watchman looking toward the dawn, who gave the example in the first place.

Postscript: As these pages were going through the press, the Vatican Council's Constitution on Divine Revelation was promulgated by His Holiness Pope Paul VI. Taken in conjunction with the earlier Instruction concerning the Historical Truth of the Gospels issued by the Pontifical Biblical Commission in 1964 with the same Holy Father's approval, this latest formulation of Catholic teaching in biblical matters leaves scholarship within the Church in full and grateful possession of its heritage from Père Lagrange, and of the rich increment that has followed from it.

3: THE PENTATEUCH: AN APPRAISAL In a testimonial to Père Lagrange written shortly after his death, the editors of the *Revue biblique* mentioned two basic characteristics of all his work: "the most rigorous honesty in his research, and complete filial submission to the Magisterium of the Church in the exposition of the convictions he had gained."[1] As an introduction to this survey of the great scholar's developing thought on the composition of the Pentateuch, I should like to refer to two brief studies of his which will serve to illustrate these characteristics. In a review of G. Hoberg's *Moses und der Pentateuch* in 1906, Lagrange, after a fairly strong criticism, remarked with his customary frankness that, if the author's book is "an attempt to satisfy (the demands of) criticism without practicing it openly, has not the moment arrived to tackle the problem of the Pentateuch critically, in all honesty, and without looking for so many detours?"[2] In the following year he could say with equal con-

[1] *RB*, XLVII (1938), p. 162.
[2] *RB*, 2d series, III (1906), p. 139. [This is Vol. XV in the current, revised numbering of *RB* as a single series from its inception in 1892.]

viction, in his commentary on the Holy Office decree, "Lamentabili . . ." that the repudiation of errors advanced in the name of criticism is not in the least an attack on the true liberty of historical criticism.[3] Since the Bible deals with divine revelation whose full meaning can only be penetrated with divine assistance, as he insisted in the first of his famous lectures at the Institut catholique of Toulouse in 1902,[4] he saw no basic contradiction between "respect for dogma and regard for sound conscientious work. All Catholics," he said, "hold that such a combination is possible. . . ."[5]

Probably no problem of biblical criticism commanded so much attention and evoked such strong and partisan feelings during much of Lagrange's career as did that of the composition of the Pentateuch. When he began his biblical studies in earnest, toward the end of the past century, a definite solution had already been proposed that had been widely acclaimed and was to become, within a short time, the common possession of practically all non-Catholic scholars. It was the Graf-Wellhausen "documentary hypothesis." In order to evaluate properly Lagrange's own contributions in this area, it is necessary to review briefly both the solution and its subsequent fate.

[3] "Le Décret 'Lamentabili sane exitu' et la critique historique," *RB*, 2nd series, IV (1907), p. 543. [Vol. XVI, revised numbering.]

[4] M.-J. Lagrange, *Historical Criticism and the Old Testament* (2d ed.; London, 1906), pp. 21-51.

[5] *Ibid.*, p. 17.

The documentary hypothesis rested upon two foundations: a literary analysis of the first five books of the Old Testament, and a philosophical conviction regarding the development of religion in general and the religion of Israel in particular. The first is, evidently, a scientific procedure; the second is a postulate. By virtue of the scientific analysis it was determined that the Pentateuch was composed of four originally distinct documents whose date and place of composition could be pinpointed by means that were, at least to some degree, critical. The Yahwist document was a ninth-century work from Judah, the Elohist document an eighth-century work from northern Israel, the Deuteronomist document a late seventh-century result of Josiah's reforming zeal, and the Priestly document a fifth-century product of the postexilic priestly school. By virtue of the philosophical postulate it was believed that the contents of the documents properly reflected, in the light of this relative chronology and provenience, the *natural* evolution of Israel's religious concepts. Accordingly, little or no concern was had for a possible predocumentary or even preliterary stage in the development of the documents, and interpretations were forced on pertinent passages to make them bring out more clearly the historical and philosophical presuppositions involved. The enigma of Israel's unique religion had been solved; the myth of Moses had been exploded; scholars could now pass on to more pressing problems.

This is not the place for a detailed examination of all the factors that, in subsequent years, forced a wholesale reconsideration of the entrenched position. Suffice it to say that these factors, the results of scientific work for the most part, demanded a rejection of the philosophical and historical system that had been so gratuitously assumed, and, to a lesser extent, of the literary analysis that had been so rigorously applied, frequently to ridiculous extremes.

This does not mean—and this is important for our purposes here—that the documentary hypothesis has been totally abandoned. Practically all scholars of the present day are in agreement that the Pentateuch does contain traditions, to use Father de Vaux's favorite expression, or sources, as Lagrange would say, that reflect varying styles, vocabularies, milieux, and theological emphases. Moreover, the majority would admit that these traditions were formulated in definitive works, before their eventual redaction with one another, more or less as the documentary hypothesis had conceived it. The Yahwist tradition, therefore, is even today commonly assigned to the tenth- or ninth-century Judah, the Elohist to eighth-century Israel, the Deuteronomist to the period of Josiah, and the Priestly tradition to the postexilic epoch.

But a greatly-increased knowledge of ancient Near Eastern history and literature in all their aspects and a more cautious use of literary analysis have led to an emphasis, not so much on the final forms of these traditions, but on their prehistory as *living* traditions within Israel. All attempts to trace this prehistory back to its ultimate origin (and the general agreement of all four traditions in the essential elements of historical, religious, cultic, and juridical principles demands a single origin) can only lead to that period when Israel was constituted the people of God, a period dominated by the figure of Moses.[6] The role of Moses, therefore, as the major individual responsible for the Pentateuch has been increasingly stressed in the modern era of biblical scholarship.

Many of the factors that contributed to these thoroughly-revised conclusions were either unknown or only vaguely known in the period when Père Lagrange was engaged in Old Testament research. A realization of this will render much more significant his own investigations into the problem of Moses and the Pentateuch. The documentary hypothesis in its pristine form held sway then, and the only means available to refute its more pernicious aspects were, on the one hand, a firm credal conviction of the divine origin of Israel's religion, a conviction that rationalism would ignore, and, on the other hand, a few gleanings from the various sciences which, however, were not yet sufficient to establish firm conclusions. Never relinquishing the one, and exhaust-

[6]R. de Vaux, *Genèse* (Paris: 1951), pp. 19-20.

ing all the resources of the other, Lagrange probed. An examination of these probings reveals the remarkable insights of this pioneer scholar.

His first published article on a Pentateuchal subject was a study of the creation story in Genesis 1.[7] It appeared in 1896. Consider the background. Twenty years earlier George Smith had just made available portions of the great Akkadian creation myth, *Enuma Elish*. Scholars had noticed similarities between it and the Genesis story of creation. J. Halévy, the Jewish Orientalist, had argued for a direct borrowing by the author of Genesis. At the other extreme, the indefatigable German Jesuit, Father von Hummelauer, had published just a year earlier his commentary on Genesis in which he held flatly that Adam had been granted a vision of the creation process, a vision that was passed on, together with other traditions contained in these early chapters, to Moses.[8] This position was to prevail among Catholic authors for a long time to come.

With the keenness of insight that was to become his trademark, Lagrange argued against both extremes. The evidence, he said, was simply too slim to conclude to a direct borrowing.[9] And yet it could not have come down, word for word, from Adam; the Bible (Jos. 24:2) tells

[7]"L'Hexaméron," *RB*, V (1896), pp. 381-407.
[8]F. von Hummelauer, *Commentarius in Genesim* (Paris, 1895), pp. 19-20.
[9]Lagrange, *RB*, V (1896), p. 402.

us explicitly that the ancestors of the Hebrews were pagans. He proposed a distinction that is today an almost universally accepted principle of exegesis, a distinction between the theological teaching and the literary framework. The theological teaching of Genesis 1 is so far superior to that of pagan creation stories that a direct borrowing is out of the question. Lagrange concluded that the teaching was revealed, either to Moses or to an earlier author, but that the framework is the fruit of Semitic genius and so could have similarities to other cosmogonies.[10]

A year later Lagrange published another article, this time on the second and third chapters of Genesis.[11] Here, for the first time, he has the occasion to accept or reject the distinction of sources in the Pentateuch. He accepts it as certain, even though he admits that he is on "slippery ground" because of the temptation to multiply those sources unreasonably.[12] The basis of his acceptance is the comparison between the two stories of creation, a comparison which he carries through the rest of the book. He carefully examines the differences: the use of the divine name, the whole series of parallel narratives throughout Genesis, the style, the vocabulary, and the manner of presenting God in his relations with man.[13]

[10]*Ibid.*, pp. 403-6.
[11]"L'Innocence et le péché" (Gn. 2; 3:1-4), *RB*, VI (1897), pp. 341-79.
[12]*Ibid.*, p. 372.
[13]*Ibid.*, pp. 369-70.

The principle of only apparent contradictions is more readily acceptable, he says, if we accept two distinct authors with two points of view and different purposes and concepts.[14] He concluded with a statement that must have raised a few Catholic eyebrows in his day, "The documentary theory formed by this fivefold knot will be broken with difficulty."[15]

In his discussion he freely makes use of the terminology of the literary critics in distinguishing between J, E, and P, but he does so only because of the common acceptance of the terms; he does not accept all the implications. Indeed, he expresses some hesitation in even admitting J and E as separate sources. It is much more difficult, he says, to distinguish J from E than the conflated JE from the Priestly code.[16] It is interesting to note that some forty years later two scholars, Volz and Rudolph, made a serious case for the denial of E as a distinct source altogether. While few modern scholars would go this far, all would endorse the carefully-phrased statement of Lagrange.

The subject was evidently much in the air. No doubt the two articles of the Dominican scholar had done much to stir up discussion. At any rate, in August of the same year (1897), he was invited to give a lecture at the Catholic Congress in Fribourg on the sources of

[14]*Ibid.*, p. 371.
[15]*Ibid.*, p. 370.
[16]*Ibid.*, p. 369.

the Pentateuch. It was published in the first issue of the *Revue biblique* of 1898.[17] The article is of extreme importance, not only for the study of Lagrange's thought, but also for the many insights it affords into problems that still trouble sincere Christians today. This is true because the article is not so much a defense of any one position as it is a closely-reasoned examination of the objections that were made, and are still being made, to critical scholarship in this and other fields. In answering these objections he makes observations that are remarkably penetrating and still valid.

After an opening appeal for Catholic tolerance, in which he says that the intellectual world cannot be forsaken by the Church,[18] he proceeds to the first objection. It is based on our modern concept of the inviolability of an author and of repugnance to successive and extensive reactions of material over a long period of time, especially when it involves the inspired word. But this, Lagrange insists, is a classical and Massoretic concept which we have inherited and which was not shared by the peoples of the ancient Near East. They practiced community in thought and in the written word as much as in social organization. Josephus is a prime extrabiblical example. And the fusing in the Massoretic text of passages that are parallel in the Septuagint shows that editorial work on the inspired books was

[17]"Les Sources du Pentateuque," *RB,* VII (1898), pp. 10-32.
[18]*Ibid.,* p. 14.

going on at a late date. If the Old Testament text had not yet reached that sacrosanct stage presumed by the Massoretes, what must have been its fate before that period?[19]

But, it is objected, if Moses is the great lawgiver of Israel, it would seem dangerous to posit evolution in the legislative section which constitutes so much of the Pentateuch. Lagrange answers that, except with regard to moral law, legislative evolution is in conformity with nature. Law governs concrete, historical man, not metaphysical man, and the historical scene changes. Even with a divine law there can be successive applications. Certain Pentateuchal laws clearly demonstrate this (for example, those concerning plurality of sanctuaries, permitted in an earlier period, but forbidden in a later). If the proposed solution, that is, legislative evolution, is not admitted, then we are faced with the Mosaic permission for many altars, on the one hand, and prohibition of them on the other. It is only to preserve the Mosaic authenticity of the whole Pentateuch that a reasonable solution is not accepted.[20]

The formula "God said to Moses" must be properly understood. It means simply that a law has emanated from the divine authority in the spirit of the first legislator, whether immediately or mediately. The formula, therefore, is a justifiable fiction that harmonizes the

[19]*Ibid.*, pp. 14-18.
[20]*Ibid.*, pp. 18-19.

eternal aspect of law with its changing aspect. It was
used by men who recognize law as a stable element in
a community and hence as something that must be
passed along "forever."[21]

This understanding of the formula can, in fact, be
applied throughout the Pentateuch. The argument from
the testimony of the Bible itself to the Mosaic authorship, therefore, must not be pressed too far. A pseudepigraphic work, that is, one attributed to an author but
not written by him at all, can be inspired, as all would
agree, for example, concerning the Book of Wisdom.[22]
Lagrange, of course, is not saying that the Pentateuch is
completely pseudepigraphic: he is merely showing the
extremes of liberty that were actually taken in the Old
Testament period with regard to authorship.

In speaking of later *Christian* tradition concerning
Moses' role, Lagrange makes a fundamental distinction
between the historical and the literary traditions. The
former refers to Moses as the legislator of Israel and to
Mosaicism as the heart of the whole history of Israel.
The latter refers to his literary activity. The historical
role is primary; the literary flows from and is dependent
on it. It cannot be argued, therefore, as some do, that,
because Israel cannot be explained without Moses, he
wrote the Pentateuch. Moreover, in this matter of the
literary tradition, we must keep in mind the later Jewish

[21]*Ibid.*, pp. 20-21.
[22]*Ibid.*, pp. 22-23.

proclivity to trace everything back to Moses, including the vowel points! Many Christians, unacquainted with Oriental practice, were taken in by this.[23]

The final and most basic objection is especially apologetic in nature. If Moses did not write the Pentateuch, how can we be assured of its historical validity? Here, it seems to me, Lagrange is at his best. First, he notes that, if a later redactor who used ancient sources is suspect in his treatment of history, would not Moses himself be suspect in his reconstruction of the history of the Patriarchs, and, all the more, of the prehistory of Genesis 1-11? Moreover, if we posit a redactor who used three witnesses to the same historical facts, the case for Israel's early history would be much stronger than if we had only one witness.[24]

A special problem is posed by the Priestly source. If this is simply another form of the history contained in J and E, then its details cannot be accepted; P has altered the truth. The principle for the solution is the same as that for the solution of the problem of the first chapters of Genesis. In the one source we have primitive history, in the other idealized history. In both, the basic historical facts are taught by means of accidental forms which are not proposed as true in themselves. The divine Author, like the human author, makes use of the details as instruments of a higher

[23]*Ibid.*, pp. 24-27.
[24]*Ibid.*, pp. 28-29.

teaching. A categorical affirmation is simply not verifiable in every line, as the chronologies of P make clear. The numbers have been handed down differently in different texts. If they had been proposed originally as strictly true, then we just do not know what the facts are. If they are only symbolic, then numerical precision is not essential. The elements to which the historical periods have been reduced are still discernible.[25] (His argument here basically is that it is safer and more logical to assume that the change has been in the accidents rather than in the substance of the text.)

In his conclusion to the lecture, Lagrange notes that he has proposed solutions guaranteeing the veracity of the Bible in any hypothesis critically acceptable. I doubt if any scholar today could find fault with any of these solutions. Indeed, it is sometimes difficult to understand how later authors, especially Catholic authors, could have failed to take notice of them. But then, we are fortunate to be working in a period when the evidence for these solutions is much clearer, a period that Père Lagrange anticipated by several generations.

Some of Lagrange's most telling remarks are made in his reviews of larger works. Thus, in his review of Hummelauer's commentary on Exodus and Leviticus,[26] he notes with satisfaction that the author is agreed that

[25]*Ibid.*, pp. 30-32.
[26]F. von Hummelauer, "Commentarius in Exodum et Leviticum," *RB*, VII (1898), pp. 136-38.

there are several sources in the Pentateuch. At least, then, the law developed in Israel and was not dropped down in one literary block from heaven! But he questions Hummelauer's statement that these sources are all pre-Mosaic. The basic question, therefore, is whether Moses is to be considered Israel's lawgiver because he placed the foundation or because he crowned the edifice. (This is a brilliant statement of the position, not only because it adequately presents the two views, but also because the figure chosen brings out clearly the relative importance of Moses' contribution in both views.) A study of the evolution of the Pentateuchal laws favors the former. That evolution is much more in conformity with Israel's history up to the time of the Babylonian captivity than with the patriarchal history.[27]

Again, in his review of the same author's commentary on Numbers,[28] he shows himself even more convinced of the necessity of literary criticism. A case in point is his comment on the Jesuit scholar's treatment of the story of Balaam. That the differences can be explained by a gloss is hardly admissible. Literary criticism says simply that there are two accounts, one by the Yahwist and one by the Elohist, that were later conflated and that basically agree. Of course, Lagrange notes, Hummelauer does not deny the existence of sources, but

[27]*Loc. cit.*
[28]F. von Hummelauer, "Commentarius in Numeros," *RB*, VIII (1899), pp. 609-13.

"one has to smile when he dates them from Adam, Noe, and Abraham."[29]

In the "Bulletin" of that same year, 1899,[30] he summarizes and comments on various studies of the literary critics and shows that he has not swallowed the whole system uncritically. Especially is he convinced that their reconstruction of the history of the Mosaic period is untenable. Yet, he can see through the presuppositions of the "school" to those elements that are soundly based. He lists them as these: the identification of Deuteronomy as a distinct work; the determination of the Priestly Code as a separate work; and the existence of a parallel account called the Elohist-Yahwist. With regard to the last two, he says, as would any modern scholar, that, while the distinction between them is not always clear, their existence as two sources is not contested.[31] That paragraph could appear in the most recent introduction to the Pentateuch.

Lagrange always found difficulty with E. By this time he was convinced that it was a distinct source, but he was also even more convinced that it was prior to, not later than, J. This was contrary to the opinion of the scholars of that day, and, of course, to the general agreement in modern scholarship, but the Dominican was firm. "We think," he wrote, "that the priority of the

[29]*Ibid.*, p. 610.
[30]Cf. *RB*, VIII, pp. 623-32.
[31]*Ibid.*, p. 630.

Elohist is one of the most solid bases of documentary and historical criticism."[32] In reading the arguments for his conviction, one is tempted to think that he was swayed somewhat by the rather cavalier way in which the critics dismissed the historical value of E. He was at pains to show that E indicates clearly that the author had before his eyes documents written by Moses.[33] Perhaps if the historical question had not been so prominent, Lagrange's view of the literary problem would not have been so firm. But this is, on the whole, a relatively minor point. What might be emphasized here, in order to evaluate the last article written by him on the subject, is his supposition that the Elohist document was composed *after* Moses' time.

Lagrange had to deal, not only with the extreme positions of the critics, but also—and this he must have felt more personally—with the attacks of his fellow Catholic scholars. Frequently in this same "Bulletin" he refers to the apologists who asked for proof of the documentary theory as though it were "like learning Arabic in twenty easy lessons."[34] We must, he said, harmonize the differences in the accounts, differences that have been noted for a long time. True literary criticism succeeds in doing this, while at the same time maintaining history in its traditional lines. This will

[32]*Ibid.*, p. 626.
[33]*Ibid.*, p. 629.
[34]*Ibid.*, p. 632.

show that the divine teaching was not a "rigid tableau that had to be learned by heart by souls unable to understand it, but . . . a light which is raised in the darkness and which continues to grow."[35]

Lagrange never did get down to a thorough analysis of all the arguments in favor of the documentary theory. He seems to suppose that they were sufficiently familiar to his readers, and they probably were. Only in articles on particular passages in the Pentateuch, such as the two stories of creation which we have already considered, does he give his reasons, and they are sound ones, for concluding to the distinction of sources. And nowhere does he treat *ex professo* the actual date of final composition of these sources or their respective milieux. Rather, he feels the need, as we have seen throughout this survey, to show not only that sound literary criticism does not deny the historical value of Moses' role, but also that it is the only reasonable explanation of the facts. And he is impatient with anyone who is careless in the application of principles. Thus, when Hummelauer, whose successive commentaries on the Pentateuch provided him with more than enough occasions for his sorties, declared that the whole character of the Deuteronomic material is post-Mosaic, he says that many false conclusions could be drawn from this. The essence of many of the laws is in fact pre-Mosaic. Actually, Lagrange would not deny the later composition of the

[35]*Loc. cit.*

Book; but he does want to insist on the long predocumentary history of the legislation. He is not, therefore, concerned to know just how many lines Moses did or did not write.[36]

Several articles and reviews followed in the years between 1901 and 1907 in which the principles of literary criticism, already accepted by Lagrange, were restated and applied. These were the years, as all know, when the criticism of modernistic tendencies was gradually reaching a point of outright and official denunciation. As several of the articles in one of the books edited by Father Murphy point out,[37] there were those who included the Dominican scholar in the denunciation. This unjust accusation did not affect his studies. He had already defended his position and felt that he was perfectly justified in continuing his scientific work. Precisely how he would have developed his Pentateuchal principles if he had continued to work in the Old Testament is an interesting question, but it cannot detain us here. Circumstances determined his invasion of the New Testament field of biblical studies where he was to gain an even greater reputation.

But the Old Testament, and the Pentateuchal problem in particular, was not forgotten by him. In fact, the last article to come from his hand concerned the

[36]F. von Hummelauer, "Commentarius in Deuteronomium," *RB*, X (1901), pp. 609-16.

[37]*Père Lagrange and the Scriptures*, ed., Richard Murphy (Milwaukee: Bruce, 1946).

Mosaic authenticity of Genesis and the documentary theory.[38] The article was written in the shadow of the Biblical Commission decree, which Lagrange quotes at the beginning. It had stated that we must accept Moses as the author of the greatest part of the Pentateuch, but that Moses could have used written or oral sources, and that some later additions can be admitted.[39] Lagrange is obviously writing from a defensive position. He did this, it is true, frequently in his career, and it resulted in some of his most discerning insights. But now he is faced with an official, though not infallible, statement of the Church.

First, he examines the recent solutions of two Catholic scholars to the admitted divergences in the Pentateuchal material, and he finds them wanting. Bea's appeal to the Semitic penchant for parallelism, which would explain the divergences while preserving the unity of authorship, is justified for poetry or recitations, but not in historical texts, especially where the style is distinct.[40] Vaccari, on the other hand, suggested that Moses wrote the whole of the Pentateuch, and that this work was later scattered among various elements of Jewish society which introduced the variations in names, style, etc. A later redaction would show all these influences. Lagrange replies

[38]"L'authenticité mosaïque de la Genèse et la théorie des documents," *RB*, XLVII (1938), pp. 163-83.
[39] *Ibid.*, pp. 163-64.
[40]*Ibid.*, pp. 167-69.

that this solution is much more narrow than that allowed by the decree and that it leads, ultimately, to this, that the canonical Pentateuch is the badly corrected fruit of flagrant instances of license taken by copyists.[41]

His own solution begins with a consideration of the revelation of the name "Yahweh" to Moses on Sinai. Quite briefly his argument is this. Since God was known as "El" before this time, the document or tradition that would have been known to Moses would understandably have been the one which referred to God as "El" in the earlier stories of the Patriarchs. (We must remember that he is mainly concerned with Genesis here.) The J or Yahwist document, which used "Yahweh" for the earlier period and which, moreover, takes history back to its beginnings, must have been composed after the revelation of the name, and therefore by Moses, or at least by a contemporary and approved by him.

He then adduces arguments to show that the preservation of these early traditions is in accord with the nature of Israel as a people; and as nomads themselves they would have recalled the wanderings of their ancestors in the land that was the object of divine promise. The most natural place for the revival and preservation of ancient traditions would be exile, when the hopes for delivery are strongest. Why, then, could

[41]*Ibid.*, pp. 169-73.

they not have been written in Egypt? Lagrange thinks
that the same method could be applied to the rest of
the Pentateuch, but he does little more than say that
P can be considered Mosaic in the sense determined
by the Commission decree.[42]

The remainder of the article considers objections
against the priority of E, against the attribution of
two parallel histories to Moses, and against the pre-
conquest origin of the documents, especially of E.[43]

The first reaction on reading the article is one of
disappointment. He had stated before, as we saw,
that E must have had before him documents written
by Moses. This, of course, supposes that the final
form of E was post-Mosaic. And, since he had always
argued for the priority of E, it also supposes that J
is, *a fortiori*, post-Mosaic. Now he is defending a
much earlier date for both these documents. And
it must be admitted that his arguments are not all
convincing. When, for example, he says that the
knowledge of the geography of Canaan, as evidenced
in J and especially in E, could, for the most part,
have been gained by a guided tour of the trans-Jordan
plateau,[44] one is not too greatly impressed. Hence,
the reader could conclude, falsely, that the great
scholar had abandoned his historico-critical method-

[42]*Ibid.*, pp. 174-79.
[43]*Ibid.*, pp. 179-83.
[44]*Ibid.*, pp. 182-83.

ology altogether and opted for the "traditional" opinion.

Actually, the only point on which he has changed his views, if it can be called a real change, is on the date of the composition of J and E of Genesis. It is his Mosaic dating of these that leads him to make the statements that are difficult to accept. And he had never really made any firm decision before this on their time of composition, even though we might legitimately infer that he had held for a post-Mosaic date. But he has not changed in the question of the distinction of sources in the Pentateuch, which is the basis of the documentary hypothesis. Nor has he changed in the question of the evolution of legislation. Where he does refer to the legal sections in this article, as in the case of P, he believes that the critical position is tenable in the face of the Commission decree. Likely he would have said the same thing with regard to Deuteronomy. And even in the dating of J and E of Genesis, it must be confessed that his arguments are, for the most part, to the point, once granted the Mosaic period as a *terminus ad quem*.

We may feel that it is unfortunate that Père Lagrange did not live to see and read the *Divino afflante Spiritu* of Pope Pius XII or the later declarations on the Pentateuch, of the Biblical Commission, documents that his own work had done so much to prepare. But this survey of his thoughts on the composition of the Pentateuch will indicate how far ahead of his time he was. And when we realize that those thoughts, formed in a time of crisis for biblical studies, were not mere intuitions, but based on the most rigorous application of scientific methods, our admiration for him is increased. It is doubtful whether he would have wanted, much less needed, any later justification. Fidelity to his intellectual principles and loyalty to his Church were sufficient justification for all he did.

4: THE PROPHETS It is a truism that the man who is ahead of his time is destined to be misunderstood in his generation. This fact rarely results in tragedy—more rarely, indeed, than we might imagine—since the truly great man is prepared for his destiny as the price he must pay for greatness; and, of course it is usually the truly great men who are ahead of their times. When tragedy occurs it is likely to involve the isolated genius who does not possess greatness. Here we might be reminded of Alfred Loisy, whose career has so often, and so superficially, been compared to that of Père Lagrange: Loisy, the fallen archangel of the biblical renaissance, whose saddest of all destines it was to find himself as ignored by the critics as he had been rejected by the Church.

We can see them together, Loisy and Lagrange, in the 1896 volume of the *Revue biblique,* Loisy writing on the synoptic apocalypse, Lagrange on inspiration, Loisy reviewing Cornill's *Jeremiah,* Lagrange discussing the Hexaemeron. Of the two, Loisy at this instant gives the impression of the stout traditionalist, Lagrange of the scholar that he always remained, never reluctant to bring forward for new discussion even the most

delicate—and, from one point of view, the most dangerous—of the biblical issues that then troubled Catholic
consciousness, issues which he faced with both an
intrepid faith and a scrupulous critical honesty. Six
years later in the same review Lagrange is assaying
Loisy's work on the Babylonian myths and the first
chapters of Genesis, a series of lectures which had been
given the year before at the École des hautes études of
Paris. The storm clouds were then already gathering
round Loisy's head, partly because they had been stirred
up by the tensions of the times, partly because Loisy
himself had seeded the storm. Lagrange's review is
typical of Lagrange: he finds Loisy wanting in good
critical method, an imperfect imitator of Holzinger and
Gunkel whose views he had popularized for his students.
In particular, he objects to Loisy's assumption that the
time was ripe for a new "general perspective," even
though based on admittedly "imperfect hypotheses."
Rather, said Lagrange: "The best means of convincing
our adversaries would be to confront them with meticulously accurate studies of details. Such studies, which
would allow sincere minds to form an opinion for themselves, would make it understandable to our own that
new things are not always dangerous things."

"Our adversaries . . ." wrote Lagrange. He knew
very well that he and all the others who had labored so
patiently and with such Catholic devotion for an *école
large* in biblical studies would be unable to escape

entirely from being tarred with the brush that Loisy had handed to its opponents, that there would be, in the words of Joseph Bonsirven, "black terror, inevitable reaction against the menace of corruption by violence, and, on this account, a long delay in the progress of Catholic biblical study." He knew, and he was to experience the knowledge throughout the rest of his life, that many would find it quite impossible to assure themselves that new things are not always dangerous things. Nevertheless, this knowledge and his experience never wrought a personal tragedy in the life of Père Lagrange, for his was a life of greatness. It also helped, of course, that it was likewise the life of a saint. I am sure that the sometimes melancholy story that was to follow can disturb us today far more than it ever could the serene faith of that obedient son of the Church who was the subject of so much of it.

The tragedy which can, however, befall a man like Père Lagrange—or a Vincent de Paul, a Thomas Aquinas, a John Henry Newman, a Francis of Assisi, name whatever giant of the past that comes to mind— is the tragedy that he cannot control because it is not of his lifetime, the tragedy, namely, that a brave man who challenges the complacency of his own age may be made the patron saint of the timid men who follow him and who are prepared to fight only the battles he has already won for them. We have heard it said many times that the radicalism of one generation is the conservatism of the next. This saying has been often abused, but it contains its truth. George Bernard Shaw may have totally misconstrued the character of the heroine of his *Saint Joan,* but the old blasphemer (I intend no moral or theological judgment here) is too close to the realities for our comfort when in the final scenes of his play he records the horror of some of the saint's clients at the thought that she might reappear on earth. We will have to admit, I am afraid, that the living presence of some of our dead heroes would often embarrass us, since this living presence would needle us quite as much as it needled its contemporaries. There is nothing particularly shameful in our making this admission, for we do not claim to be better men than our fathers were, and we venerate our heroes precisely because they were better men.

However, if we intend to honor Père Lagrange as he deserves to be honored, it will be by perpetuating his greatness less in memorials than in the imitation of his faith in God, his loyalty to the Church, and his insatiable intellectual curiosity concerning the things of God and man, especially as they are found in Sacred Scripture where God and man meet. When we page through the truly amazing record of Lagrange's literary life compiled by Père Braun in the book Father Murphy has made available to the English-speaking world—over eighty-five closely printed pages of titles, some 1,786 in all—we can hardly find an entry all the way from

1892 till 1938 that does not deal with an issue that was both living and controversial. We shall always want to ask the question: *Quid dixit magister?*—What did the master say?—for Père Lagrange was incapable of saying anything trivial or inconsequential. But even more we shall want to ask: *Quid docuit magister?*—What did the master teach us? How and to what purpose did he say what he said? What has he left for us to say? And how are we to say it, if we would speak in this year of grace with a voice like to his in his own year?

When we come to Père Lagrange and the prophets, we can find answers to both these questions, I believe, in the very first volume of the *Revue biblique*, that of 1892, in which there are two articles with themes that were to engage Lagrange's attention much of his life. The first of these articles is entitled "The New History of Israel and the Prophet Hosea"; the second, "The Virgin and Immanuel."

By the "new history of Israel" Lagrange meant the naturalized history without revelation, without miracles, and without prophecies, as told by Kuenen, Wellhausen, and Renan, which had now been popularized and had attained textbook status. In this history the unique character of Israel in the ancient world was prominently featured; it was even exaggerated, to disastrous conclusions. For, according to these masters, the Israelite Yahweh, originally a local deity, a nature god who had obtained a position of monolatry among this people, had been transformed by degrees, in response to historical circumstances entirely intra-Israelite, into the monotheistic God of the Old Testament and of later Christianity. This transformation was the work of the prophets, those solitary religious geniuses who had literally snatched victory—a victory theretofore unheard of —from the jaws of national defeat, by reinterpreting Israelite history and religion and imposing on both a moral theology. Whereas Israel, in bowing to the superior might of the Assyrian juggernaut, should have adapted to the common pattern which demanded that its national god be regarded as a conquered god and therefore a no-god, the prophets had intervened to explain Israel's disgrace as due not to Yahweh's weakness but to his power; the Assyrians were Yahweh's instrument, punishing his people for covenant violation. Yahweh's power was supreme, not only over Israel but also over Assyria. This was the birth of ethical monotheism.

Lagrange criticized this new history on the solid grounds that it had begun with an hypothesis taken from without the Bible to which it had then adjusted the biblical evidence, discarding whatever could not be fitted into its pattern. He continually protested that the obvious sense of the biblical texts was something far different from what they were being made to say in obedience to this hypothesis. Modern biblical scholarship is all on the side of Lagrange. There are several judgments of fact made in the course of the article which could hardly be sustained today—nor, for that matter, would Lagrange attempt to sustain them today—but they are peripheral to the main issue. What Lagrange had to say on the main issue could hardly be better said even now.

Another presupposition opposed in this article, a contention that Lagrange aptly called "the preferred subject of the evolutionary school," was that prophetic and priestly religion were originally thesis and antithesis, that the synthesis that finally resulted was late, as represented, for example, in the Law of Holiness (that is, Leviticus 17-26) of the priestly legislation, that, above all, it was the religion of Israel itself and not deviations from it that the prophets condemned in the name of a newly-revealed moral deity. Lagrange sent Wellhausen back to the prophetic texts—in this article he was mainly concerned with the prophet Hosea—which the great German scholar had studied with such amazing erudition but so little understanding. That the prophets charged Israel with disobedience, he reasonably pointed out, proves the existence of a law, not its non-existence. Subsequent biblical study was to agree with him.

The "new history of Israel" is now a thing of the past: Lagrange in 1892 could hardly have surmised how quickly it would go into the critical discard. Why it would do so, however, he certainly understood. Today

the standard textbook treatment of the history of Israel
is likely to be that of Martin Noth or of John Bright,
approaches that display considerable divergence, it is
true, but which concur in all essentials against the
Histoire du peuple d'Israel of Ernest Renan or the
Israelitische und jüdische Geschichte of Julius Wellhausen. Certain new discoveries, mainly the contributions of biblical archaeology, have helped to bring about
this change; but far more important has been the con-
tinuous and patient examination of the text insisted on
by Père Lagrange, in the light of which presuppositions
that were never soundly critical have been unable to
survive.

The early relation of law to cult in Israelite religion
was demonstrated, for example, by Sigmund Mowinckel's literary and form-critical study of the Decalogue
in 1927. In 1930 Martin Noth published his work on
the tribal system of Israel, showing that the covenant
community, far from being the theological afterthought
that Wellhausen made of it, had its roots in the pre-
monarchical period of Israelite history, precisely where
the Bible places it. The masterful study of the origins
of Israelite law published by Albrecht Alt in 1934
examined the Mosaic codes from the standpoint of
what was derivative and what was unique in their
legislation, and pointed to the antiquity of both legal
forms, the casuistic and the apodictic. Two studies by
Professor George Mendenhall of the University of

Michigan in 1954, one on Israelite law and the other on Israelite covenant forms, have encouraged several subsequent scholars following in his wake to set the origins of what Wellhausen would have called the prophetic religion squarely in the Mosaic age. Meanwhile, studies on the nature and phenomenology of prophetism by scholars far too numerous to name—Mowinckel and a substantial Scandinavian school, Alfred Guillaume, and countless others—have destroyed the illusion of the cultural vacuum in which Israel was alleged to have elaborated its vision of God. In doing so, they have underscored what was really unique in Israel, its dynamic religion, that produced alike the glory of its prophetism and the majesty of its law.

The other article of 1892, on the Virgin and the Immanuel of Isaiah, is perhaps instructive of how we may learn from Père Lagrange without being compelled to follow all his conclusions. Biblical messianism was one of Lagrange's lifelong interests, but I think it is safe to say that this is an area of biblical study in which his thought never achieved the final maturation that he desired of it. In part this was doubtless due to the long interruption of his Old Testament studies; though, on the other hand, his study of the New Testament during this period, which turned out to be some of the most important work he ever did, only served to sharpen an awareness he had shown from the beginning, namely, of the extreme complexity of the

Old Testament messianic expectation, and the corresponding fulfillment of it claimed in the New Testament. The complications of intertestamental Jewish messianism that grew out of the Old Testament were meticulously detailed by Lagrange in his book *Le messianisme chez les Juifs* published in 1909, a work which remains one of the classic studies of the subject.

Both before and since Lagrange, Catholic theologians have all too frequently adopted a *simpliste* attitude towards biblical messianism. Especially in the area of popular apologetics and even, unfortunately, in some manuals that claim to be laying the groundwork for a scientific theology, we are still too often confronted by what is confidently called an "argument from prophecy" consisting of a concatenation of Old Testament texts listed without reference to context or historical authorship, but only as regards their supposed content, which is then systematically paralleled with a portrait of Jesus Christ derived from the New Testament. The principle that has governed the selection of these texts is, mainly, that they are the Old Testament *testimonia* exploited by the New Testament, where, however, they do not appear as apologetical arguments but as integrated into Christian preaching and teaching, as already read, therefore, in the light of New Testament faith. Even at its best, consequently, this argument is likely to appear to the disinterested observer as a studied exercise of reasoning in a circle. By its very naïveté, its presumption that there are seventy-five or so Old Testament texts—to elucidate the precise historical sense of which we should require at least as many volumes—which conspire to make up a portrait that is ineluctably that of Jesus Christ, that the "argument from prophecy" which somehow has escaped a number of the keenest minds of the past and present is in reality a kind of elementary jigsaw puzzle that can be assembled by a routine paging of the Bible over an idle half hour or so—all this, far from illustrating the reasonableness of the Christian faith, can only provoke those *irrisiones infidelium,* the scandal of the educated unbeliever, which were the dread of Augustine, of Thomas Aquinas, of Cardinal Newman, and of Père Lagrange.

What is radically wrong in this approach to messianism, however, is the travesty it makes of biblical prophecy and of the relation of the Old Testament to the New. It was here that Lagrange attacked it, in the name of a messianology that could be both scientifically justified and genuinely Christian. Blaise Pascal is one of those who have been credited with the development of the modern messianic apologetic argument. In a conference at St. Stephen's published in 1906 Lagrange made a searching investigation into Pascal's teaching, acknowledging the errors in fact and methodology, but exonerating the great apologist of the basic misconceptions that have just been mentioned. He also found in the substance of Pascal's argument an essential validity which he commended to the attention of theologians. It should be noted that, as outlined by Lagrange, this exposition has, in point of fact, been increasingly stressed in modern theology, particularly as the shortcomings of the "proof-text" method have been made and more obvious. By a semantic peculiarity not unknown elsewhere in theology, however, it is likely to be called the "new" as opposed to the "traditional" messianology, though, as we have just said, Lagrange ascribed it to Pascal, both in the 1906 conference and in a 1917 review of Touzard's article on Old Testament Judaism in the *Dictionnaire apologétique de la Foi Catholique,* and, for that matter, did not hesitate to identify it with the messianism in the apostolic kerygma of the New Testament. "Proof-text messianology," on the other hand, at least in its full-blown form, is hardly older than the work of Christian Pesch following the First Vatican Council.

While Pascal himself had attached some importance to supposed prophecies of detail concerning the life of Christ, he had been very much aware of the obscurity and contrariety that characterize biblical prophecy; furthermore, he was too much the mathematician to be highly impressed by the mechanical law of probability which Pesch was to think he could discern in such prophecies. Lagrange, of course, was able to confirm Pascal's misgivings many times over in the light of the critical study of the Bible. The fact had to be recognized, as Pascal had recognized it in principle, that for every one of the prophets the predicted Savior had quite exceeded the expectation. This fact, which of itself invalidated the assumption that any list of Old Testament texts could ever add up to a finished portrait of Christ, was no new discovery, Lagrange repeatedly reminded his readers. As St. Jerome had said: "It is the one thing to know in the Spirit what will take place, and another to see it when it has taken place . . . just as it is one thing to hold something in one's hands, and another to foresee it in spirit." And Paul himself had written of the mystery of Christ as "in other ages . . . not known to the sons of men as it has now been revealed to his holy apostles and prophets in the Spirit" (Eph. 3:5-6). The fulfillment of the messianic hope, both Pascal and Lagrange knew, without contradicting the spirit of the Old Testament prophecies, nevertheless far transcended it.

Still, from the first preaching of Christianity the hearer of the word had been invited to discern in the New Testament realities the outlines of an Old Testament pattern. How was the connection between the two to be shown: by what principle could it be said that the latter was a prophecy of the former? Pascal's solution was his doctrine of the two senses of prophecy. The prophets, he said, had consciously spoken in figures, intending their words, which were formed in the thought patterns and within the horizons of ancient

Israel, to find their proper application in the new law and the new covenant of the New Testament.

Lagrange knew that this solution could not stand. "No Jewish prophet could have received such a mission," he stated. "How could God have urged the execution of a law condemned in advance as imperfect?" In all his work on the prophets he constantly and rightly insisted that the prophets must be understood in terms of the Israel to whom they had been sent, as sharing its legitimate aspirations and having central to their thoughts its contemporary concerns, including, of necessity, its limitations as well. An article he had prepared that same year (1906) on the messianic prophecies of the last Israelite prophets is illustrative of Lagrange's approach, the only scientifically justifiable approach. If, then, as he would agree, there was a dimension to the prophetic word that made it applicable, properly applicable, to the economy of salvation as proclaimed by the New Testament, it must not be found by making the prophecies read ambiguously.

Lagrange found it in the very historical study of the Bible which had shown some of the older approaches to prophecy to be invalid. The Old Testament revelation was the product of a divine condescension measured out over many centuries, ending in a kaleidoscope of theologies, that is to say, in the responses which the mind of man makes to revelation. Through it all there is a marvelous thread of continuity. The Pentateuchal traditions, for example, extend throughout nearly the whole of historical Israel; some of them can be traced back to the very origins of Israel and can even be lost in the mists of the past when there was no Israel, while others quite clearly belong to the divine action in history which brought forth Judaism after the Babylonian captivity. Still, not even the most radical critic would suggest that there is anything other than a single Pentateuch, even though he might prefer today to call it by another name. There has been throughout all these centuries a basic preservation of type, together with an extraordinary diversity and development. And so it has been with the New Testament fulfillment of the Old; this, in fact, is what we really mean by New Testament fulfillment: diversity, development, preservation of type. As Father John McKenzie has put it:

> One's hope can be fulfilled. One's personality or destiny can be fulfilled by the realization of the potentialities which lie within one's person. One's desires can be fulfilled. In all of these the common element is the emergence of some reality which in some way is foreshadowed, demanded, needed by that which precedes it: a reality without which the preceding unreality remains unfulfilled and to that extent unreal. Jesus is the reality which gives fullness to the reality of the Old Testament; he satisfies its desires, realizes its hopes and potentialities, gives it intelligibility. He is the fullness of Israel.

The prophets play their role in the divine economy not as soothsayers and fortunetellers but as mouths for the word of God by which, little by little, and sometimes in quite contrasting ways, the kingdom of God is proclaimed, always adequately in relation to its place in the history of salvation, yet ever incompletely, with an incompleteness that is revealed by each successive new stage in this history. And when the history at last reaches its goal—which is, in turn, the beginning of another and totally unexpected phase of the same history —and only when it reaches its goal, the role played by each prophet can be exactly measured as it figured in the grand design, the continuity which unites this history and was of no human fashioning. This is the true argument from prophecy. This is what the author of the Epistle to the Hebrews meant, as he is translated in the New English Bible: "When in former times God spoke to our forefathers, he spoke in fragmentary and varied fashion through the prophets. But in this the final age he has spoken to us in the Son whom he has made heir to the whole universe. . . ."

I suggested above that Père Lagrange never brought his thinking on prophetic messianism to full maturity. It was not, as I am sure we have seen, through any need to refine his principles. Lagrange's own consistency in this respect amounts at times almost to a *tour de force,* as, for example, when we see him return in 1930 to a study he had made in 1904 on the so-called prophecy of the seventy weeks in the Book of Daniel. It would be a rare person indeed who, after twenty-six years—a short lifetime, after all—would find as little that really required changing as Lagrange did in this instance. If he suffered from any limitations, they were mainly those of his time, which dictated that a disproportionate attention be given to apologetical concerns; he was hardly ever able to write without the need to have his eye peeled for the enthusiast of either the left or the right who would try to make too little or too much of the biblical evidence. His work was done in a time of crisis when there was too little of that serenity that is necessary climate for productive scholarship. The same apologetical preoccupations, as we know, characterize his great commentaries on the Gospels, which remain monuments of critical philology. If today we possess more of that serenity he lacked, which has been signaled for us above all in the *Divino afflante Spiritu* of 1943, it is due, of course, to the patience and sacrifices of men like Père Lagrange.

Prophetical messianism, both in the area of apologetics and as a department of theology in its own right, is still very much a living issue in Catholic scholarship. Most of the questions that were being asked in Lagrange's time are still being asked, and new questions have been raised as they have been provoked by a broader and deeper knowledge of the ancient Near East and the comparative study of its religions. Some of the new dimensions of this study may be seen treated in the 1957 volume of the *Catholic Biblical Quarterly*, in which were gathered the more important papers delivered at the 1956 annual meeting of the Catholic Biblical Association which was entirely devoted to this topic; also in *L'attente du Messie,* edited by Canon Joseph Coppens and published in 1954, the record of one of the famous *journées bibliques* of Louvain University similarly given over exclusively to this all-important subject. It is safe to say that, in investigations such as these, Père Lagrange would be happy to recognize the continued application of the principles to which he dedicated his life and talents.

Whereas in Lagrange's time the reconciliation of prophetic and priestly religion was still a point of contention, study of comparative religions in our own times has confronted us with an entirely different problem which seems at first glance to be leading to conclusions that are precisely a contradiction of the criticism of the last century. The Near Eastern pattern of prophet-priest, of cult prophet, has been set in parallel with the canonical prophets by important authors like A. R. Johnson, Alfred Haldar, and many others. In turn, this has been represented by S. H. Hooke, Sigmund Mowinckel, Ivar Engnell, and a large school of scholars in their wake as one aspect only of the myth-and-ritual pattern involving king, cult, prophet, and priest in varying degrees and functions. The relation of the cult to the monarchy, to prophecy, and to psalmody in ancient Israel has undergone and undergoes searching re-examination; and all of this obviously has a great deal to do with the interpretation of prophecy in general and with the history of messianism in particular. It is not surprising, therefore, that the synthesis Lagrange did not achieve has not been achieved in the generation that followed his death. Neither is it likely to be achieved in the generation that follows this.

Another facet of prophecy that remains obscure is that of its fulfillment in the New Testament and the Church. I have already said that Lagrange pointed the way to the solution of this question in his critique of Pascal. Although this is true for the broad outlines of the problem, nevertheless there is considerable difference of opinion concerning the details and even concerning some of the theological assertions we are required to make. If we recognize that the prophets spoke in some fashion or other of the kingdom of God, with varying degrees of understanding of what God in his mercy would bring forth, and if we believe as Christians that the kingdom of God has truly come in Jesus and that it is therefore of Jesus that the prophets spoke, still, we know very well that between the prophetic ideal even at its highest and the New Testament realization there is a separation of more than language and time. More than language and time, too, are needed to explain the tension that sometimes exists between the scriptural word and the continued life the word has found in the teaching and preaching of the Church. In what does the vitality that has effected these changes consist? Is it a vitality of word itself, which was multiplex from the outset, containing in itself a fuller sense that only needed to be unfolded in time? Or is the vitality rather in the later light that God has vouchsafed, in which can better be seen truths to which the word has witnessed adequately yet imperfectly? The hermeneutical problem remains, and I have somewhat oversimplified it by offering these rather neat alternatives. It is indicative of Lagrange's continuing influence in Catholic biblical studies, at all events, that advocates of one or the other of these positions have claimed him as their master.

If some of the problems Lagrange encountered in the prophetic literature have subsequently become more complex, others have solved themselves, or at least been seen in a perspective rather different from before. Lagrange, writing on the so-called Deutero-Isaiah in 1892 or on the Apocalypse of Isaiah (that is, chapters 24-27) in 1894, felt compelled to defend, in the name of tradition, the uncritical view that would make them the work of the eighth-century prophet Isaiah. In his later writings he considerably sharpened his appreciation of tradition and its limitations and imperatives. Meanwhile, our understanding of the meaning of authorship in the ancient Near East has become much more sophisticated. What the nineteenth-century literary critics regarded as additions and interpolations in the prophetic books, we now know are rather the record of the transmission of these books in the prophetic circles that surrounded the great prophets and preserved for posterity their originally oral utterances. Neither in respect to the prophets nor in respect to the rest of the biblical literature is literary authorship necessarily the decisive factor in determining a given passage as authentically Isaian or Jeremian or Johannine. Here we can only allude to this quite new dimension of biblical study that has been opened before us, the implications of which, for every branch of the work, we can hardly even surmise as yet.

A final area of prophetic study was never very much explored by Père Lagrange. That is the nature of prophetic inspiration itself, considered strictly as a biblical phenomenon. Our classical theological considerations of prophecy, such as Thomas Aquinas' *De prophetia* treatise, have approached the matter rather from an a priori viewpoint than from the biblical evidence. The rationalistic critics with whom we first meet Lagrange in conflict had also approached the subject in an a priori manner, though on quite different premises. The study of analogous prophetic institutions in comparative religions, to which I alluded before, together with continued study of the history and consistency of Israelitic prophetism itself, have shown us how much more needs to be thought and said in this regard. New ground needs to be broken before there can be a new grand synthesis. New ground that was not Lagrange's. But even here I think Lagrange has something to teach us: namely, his methodology, which we would do well to make our own.

Le plus sur est de s'en tenir aux textes—the safest
thing is to stick to the texts. That tells at least half the
story of Père Lagrange's scholarship. One of his greatest
virtues, from the scholarly standpoint, was the ability
to read with understanding and to know the sources he
used. A patient examiner of the evidence himself, he
had to be equally patient all his life with those who
would not or could not read it with similar understanding. If he had to send Wellhausen back to Hosea, he
also had to send the critics in his own Church back to
the many sources they had cited against him: these
included, and especially, the works of Père Lagrange
himself. The editors of one journal he had to send
back to their own earlier issues, with which they were
at war rather than with the *Revue biblique,* noting
wryly that they had achieved the greater victory which
consists in conquering oneself. He showed on more
than one occasion that he knew the Fathers far better
than those who imagined that his doctrine was something different from theirs. Such was his reply to a
book published in 1905 bearing the incredible title
Twenty-five Years of Struggle for Biblical Truth—incredible, when one discovers that in its author's mind
the chief antagonist of biblical truth during this quarter-
century had been Père Lagrange.

Stick to the texts, but read with understanding. The
author of the *Twenty-five Years of Struggle* . . . had
taken as his leitmotiv the biblical injunction: "Remove

not the ancient landmark which your fathers set up" (Prv. 22:28). As he interpreted it, this rule would have doomed Catholic scholarship not, truly, to a traditional exegesis—this, as Lagrange showed, was not really the point at issue—but to fighting battles with enemies who no longer existed, to holding redoubts against a siege that had been long abandoned, and to the proposition that human wisdom and ingenuity reached its optimum growth at a determinable point in the past, some twenty-five years before. It was no reverence for the word of God, Lagrange knew, which could inspire the thought that sound exegesis could survive only by pretending that the world of here and now did not exist. It was, rather, that feeling of insecurity with the consequences of living, which are growth and change, which manifests itself in various men in various ways. Its common manifestation in religion is to mistrust any human mind that has not been safely interred—in fact or in principle—and to extend the landmarks of faith at the expense of reason, hankering after simple and once-for-all answers to questions that God has decreed shall ever trouble the mind and conscience of man.

Stick to the evidence and question, ever question. That is what the master has taught us. To the extent that it is in this spirit Catholic biblical studies continue to move, to that extent the spirit of Père Lagrange continues to move in them.

5: PAUL AND THE INDWELLING CHRIST Concerning Protestant theology of an earlier day, Albert Schweitzer wrote this criticism: "What men looked for in Paul's writings was proof-texts for Lutheran and Reformed Theology; and that was what they found. Reformation exegesis reads its own ideas into Paul, in order to receive them back again clothed with apostolic authority."[1]

Concerning the state of Catholic exegesis and theology when Père Lagrange came on the scene, much the same could be said. Theology, on the one hand, had little concern to penetrate the thrust behind the isolated Scripture texts it used, and was satisfied in finding some justification for its own speculations. Exegesis, on the other hand, when it was really scientific, seemed more concerned with the minutiae of its auxiliary sciences than with the fullblown theological import of the sacred texts.

For the sake of those not acquainted with the technical terms—and not even theologians are agreed on precisely how to define them—it should be known that

[1] *Paul and His Interpreters*, trans. W. Montgomery (New York: Macmillan, 1956), p. 2.

a distinction is normally made between exegesis and biblical theology. Exegesis in the strict sense is the analysis of a given text for all that it is worth, but we might say also for *only* what it is worth, within the scope of the particular context in which it was written. The exegete has already made an immense contribution when he tells us, in the light of literary and historical criticism of philology, archaeology, and the other ancillary sciences he uses, what *this* text means. The biblical theologian, who, please God, will first be an exegete, wants to go beyond the limits of this or that text and seize the *total* thought of the author. This will involve a synthesis of the data of exegesis, surely, but beyond that an attempt to reconstruct the inner fabric of the writer's original intuition—what one scholar has called the "inspired theology" of the sacred author himself.

Now one of the major elements of the Catholic biblical movement today is the phenomenon of biblical theology. The appearance of this fruit of biblical research is due in great measure to the École biblique and thus ultimately to the influence of Père Lagrange.

But the precise contribution of this scholar was that he insisted on rooting biblical theology in exegesis—a principle that may be obvious today but was not so obvious to the theologians of a few decades ago. In reviewing Père Prat's *Theology of Saint Paul* (the French edition), Père Lagrange noted that the Jesuit scholar had joined to his exegesis a certain amount of speculation, and then added: "He is perhaps even more distinguished in exegesis than in speculation. But after all, what value would there be in applying speculation to St. Paul without the exegesis of his texts?" And then, with a wry smile in his pen, the reviewer adds: "And this malicious trait [speculation] in the end would be quite a good thing if it should make Père Prat decide to undertake the exegesis of the Pauline epistles *ex professo*."[2]

The apparent distaste for speculation which this remark reveals (in a review that is otherwise highly laudatory) does not mean that Père Lagrange considered exegesis an end in itself. What he was concerned with is that the construction of biblical theology be firmly rooted in a sound exegesis first of all. Once that is done, however, he maintains that Paul cannot be understood except as a theologian. To understand his thought is to penetrate his theology. In reviewing the commentary of Robertson-Plummer on 1 Corinthians, Père Lagrange writes: "We have spoken first of all of theology, because the theological question is the one which arises first when one studies St. Paul."[3]

Thus, it seems to me quite natural that when we turn to Père Lagrange's work on Paul we should speak of his contribution to biblical theology. It is true that the

[2]*RB*, XXI (1912), pp. 618-19.
[3]"Nous avons parlé tout d'abord de la théologie, qui s'impose la première quand il s'agit de Saint Paul," *RB*, XXI (1912), pp. 140-41.

needs of his day kept him more in the unexplored regions of exegesis (and in Paul chiefly in his commentaries on Romans and Galatians, which have not aged), but the works of his disciples—men like Pères Benoit, Boismard, De Vaux, and Spicq—show that their master had laid the solid foundations for biblical theology and pointed the way to it. Having been privileged to study under one of the men he formed, Père Spicq, I feel I can say this with conviction as well as with gratitude.

It is precisely a topic of Pauline theology which I should like to develop here to honor the memory of Père Lagrange: Paul and the Indwelling Christ.

We all know that one of the great themes God has written into the story of his love for man is that of his indwelling. To understand Paul's theology of the indwelling Christ, it will be necessary first of all to give a thumbnail sketch of the way in which this theology was prepared for in the Old Testament and in the teaching of Jesus.

Like so many other summits to which Jewish theology attained, the consciousness of the divine indwelling was a progressive one. To Abraham God reveals himself as a friend; he intervenes to call him and at critical moments favors him with an appearance. But with Abraham, as with the other patriarchs, God's presence is a passing one, a presence of isolated theophanies.

God's true dwelling place is in heaven, not on earth (Dt. 26:15).

In the more primitive Yahwist and Elohist accounts of the Exodus, God reveals his presence especially as an active helper who is *with* his people in the great saving acts they have experienced or who goes before them as a leader: "I will be with you" (Ex. 3:12); "My presence shall go before you" (Ex. 33:14; cf. 34:9). In the covenant struck on Sinai, God has identified himself with the interests of his people to such an extent that we can say that *where his people is, there is Yahweh*. This was not, of course, understood in such a way that Yahweh was bound to a place in the way that the surrounding pagans often thought of their local gods; no earthly image was to be made of Israel's God (Ex. 20:4-5; Dt. 5:8-10) lest he be thought to be limited thereto. But there is the idea of localization in his people, and of this type of presence the tent and the ark were the symbols. The way was therefore laid for the Priestly tradition to describe these symbols in terms of a dwelling place for God: "I will consecrate the Meeting Tent. . . . I will dwell in the midst of the Israelites and will be their God. They shall know that I, the Lord, am their God who brought them out of the land of Egypt, *so that I*, the Lord, their God, *might dwell among them*" (Ex. 29:44-46; italics added). To keep things in their proper historical perspective we should realize that this "theologizing" on the tabernacle as God's dwelling place, as well as the description of its manner of construction, the permanent presence of the cloud above it, along with the exclusive service of the Levites, all derive from the Priestly Code and their final form is postexilic. They are the direct expressions of the priestly theology of the temple restored by Zorobabel in 515 B.C. But the ease with which these later scribes reinterpret the tent and the ark shows that the basic elements for the theology of God's "tabernacling with men" were already present in the events around Sinai. The true meaning of these events and the symbols that accompanied them, the Priestly author tells us, is that God was promising and preparing a permanent dwelling place among his people.

When, much later, the thought occurs to David to build God a house, Nathan tells the king that instead God will build one for him—house here meaning dynasty, as in English we would speak of the "House of York." The central importance of this prophecy (2 Sm. 7) is that it marks the unquestionable beginning of the messianic hope in Israel. From this time forward, Israel's attention is more and more fixed on the future, and this future hope also influences the theme of the divine indwelling. Although not explicitly stated, the thought is now one of God's special presence in the *dynasty,* in the house of David.

It is David's son Solomon who actually proceeds to the building of the temple. The special significance of this event is that God's presence is no longer merely a spiritual one; it will have some sort of permanent embodiment.

When Solomon's temple was destroyed in 586 B.C. and the people were driven into exile, their faith underwent a crisis that purified and elevated their concept of the divine indwelling, complacent as it had become in the saving power of the material structure and externals of worship. Crushed by the loss of the temple, the faith of the exiles rallied and affirmed that God had gone with his people into exile: "Thus says the Lord God: Though I have removed them far among the nations and scattered them over foreign countries—and *was* for a while *their only sanctuary* in the countries to which they had gone. . ." (Ez. 11:16; italics added).

This affirmation of Ezekiel was basically the message the earlier prophets had hammered home, even before the temple went down: the place of God's dwelling is men's hearts, even if they constitute only a faithful and purified remnant (Jer. 7:1-8; 31:31-34). Yet, Ezekiel too yearned for and prophesied the restoration of the temple itself, even giving a grandiose description of it in chapters 40-43 and promising that Yahweh would return to dwell there (Ez. 43:7).

The priestly theology of the restoration then fused the two currents: God's dwelling in his people and the centralization of that indwelling in the temple—and thus reinterpreted ancient Israel's history as the preparation for this indwelling: "They shall make a sanctuary for me, that I may dwell in their midst" (Ex. 25:8 [P]). This is revealed by the two texts the Jews loved to quote as a promise of that temple to come:

"I will set my Dwelling among you, and will not disdain you. Ever present in your midst, I will be your God and you will be my people" (Lv. 26:11-12 [P]).
"I will make with them a covenant of peace; it shall be an everlasting covenant with them, and I will multiply them, and put my sanctuary among them forever. My dwelling shall be with them; I will be their God, and they shall be my people" (Ez. 37:26-27).

We know how the teaching of Jesus and the theology of the primitive Christian community pointed to the fulfillment of these prophecies in the body of Jesus himself, the clearest text being that of John 2:19-21: "'Destroy this temple, and in three days I will raise it up.' . . . He was speaking of the temple of his body." The body of Christ risen from the tomb then becomes the central place of the worship of the Father and the place where God now takes his residence among men.

With these elements hastily sketched, we are in a better position to grasp Paul's theology of indwelling.

The central and decisive experience in Paul's life—the experience which gave him the basic orientation for all his subsequent theological development—was the event on the road to Damascus. When the figure appeared to him in divine glory and said, "I am Jesus, whom thou art persecuting," Paul realized that there was an identity between the risen Christ and his members which could not be severed.

His first letter to the Thessalonians reveals, however, that at this stage Paul's thought is dominated less by the Christ present in the Church than by the Christ coming in glory to judge the living and the dead. The Thessalonians were themselves preoccupied by the problem of the Parousia, the Second Coming of Christ, and this in part explains Paul's emphasis on the theme. He does address the community as "the church of the Thessalonians [which is] in God the Father and in the Lord Jesus Christ" (1 Thes. 1:1), and later in the letter, he addresses a prayer to the Lord Jesus to give them an increase of love (1 Thes. 3:12). All this supposes a present union, but the general stress of the letter is not there. The perspective is the future, and Christian life is defined in terms of waiting the glorious return of Christ (1 Thes. 1:10). If the Christian life has moral demands, it is because there is a presence of God and Christ towards which Christians are destined, and holiness is defined as being worthy of that presence to come (1 Thes. 3:13). Paul does allude to the fact that Christians' present possession of God's Holy Spirit makes immorality all the more horrendous, but he does not press the point (1 Thes. 4:8).

We now turn to the letter to the Philippians, which, in the opinion of more and more scholars today, was written during a captivity of St. Paul at Ephesus, in the years 56-57, after the Thessalonian letters and shortly before the crisis at Corinth. Reading this warm and affectionate epistle, we notice that the perspective of the Second Coming is still strong. He speaks of the "day of Christ" (Phil. 1:10), the Lord who is soon coming (Phil. 4:5); as for us, he says, "Our native city is in heaven, from which also we eagerly await a Savior, our Lord Jesus Christ" (Phil. 3:20). But this future perspective gives meaning to present Christian suffering and to Paul's own chains, for these are borne *for* Christ (Phil. 1:13, 29). That is why Paul can say that "to live is Christ and to die is gain" (Phil. 1:21).

From the future perspective giving meaning and destiny to the present life (living *for* Christ, for his future presence, all of which was present in Thessalonians), Paul now in the Philippian letter moves into the thought of his present union with Christ: the formula "in Christ" or "in the Lord" becomes more frequent. He speaks of "comfort in Christ" or "fellowship in the Spirit" (Phil. 2:1). And above all he introduces the theme of union with the risen Christ and fellowship with the suffering Christ, when he defines the Christian life as knowing him, and what a power his resurrection is, and what it is to share his sufferings (Phil. 3:10). The goal of this union is of course still strongly stressed: becoming conformed to his death, so "that somehow I may attain to the resurrection from the dead" (Phil. 3:11).

It is in the first Epistle to the Corinthians that we begin to see how deep the present union with Christ is meant to be. The "in Christ" formulas become deeper and more theological: Christians are "*sanctified* in Christ" (1 Cor. 1:2); "*justified* in Christ" (1 Cor. 6:11). The Christ Paul preaches is specifically the crucified Christ, and, he tells the Corinthians, "You are in Christ Jesus, who has become for us God-given wisdom, and justice, and sanctification, and redemption" (1 Cor. 1:30). These statements come in the first part of the epistle which has to do with the problem of unity within the Corinthian community, torn as it was by factions, each claiming that its favorite preacher was the one to be followed. When Paul wants to stress that the ministers are only instruments, and that the community belongs to God he says, "You are God's tillage, God's *building*" (1 Cor. 3:9; italics added; see vv. 5-9). Paul does not immediately have in mind the divine indwelling when he calls Christians "God's building" here; what he wants to stress is that God is the primary builder of the community and that the community belongs to him rather than to any preacher. Christ is presented as the foundation of the building (1 Cor. 3:11), not as the indwelling Lord.

But a few lines later, Paul says: "Do you not know that you are the temple of God and that the Spirit of God dwells in you? If anyone destroys the temple of God, him will God destroy; for holy is the temple of God, and this temple you are" (1 Cor. 3:16-17). Here for the first time Paul introduces the temple theme. The word he uses is *naos,* which really means the sanctuary of the temple. So there is no doubt that he means the divine indwelling in the strictest sense of the term. Moreover, this first usage of *naos* by St. Paul is applied not to a building, nor to the mystical body of Christ, but to the Church, the Christian community. In modern spirituality the divine indwelling is thought of principally in individual terms—"God dwells in the soul," we are inclined to say. But here, it is not of the individual at all that Paul is thinking—except to condemn individualism roundly, for individualism shatters the temple of God. Paul therefore uses *temple* here to stress *the sacred unity of the people of God.* It is in this unity alone that God dwells.

Notice, in passing, that the temple which is the community is referred to the Father as its owner, to the Spirit of God as effecting the divine indwelling. Christ is not mentioned.

From the theme of unity, Paul passes on to the problem of purity. He says that Christians cannot unite with a harlot because their *bodies* are *members* of *Christ* (1 Cor. 6:15); an equivalent for this is given four verses later, when he says: "Your members are the temple of the Holy Spirit" (1 Cor. 6:19). The temple theme, which was used earlier as an exhortation to unity, is here applied to the body of the individual Christian. The Christian cannot unite himself with a harlot because he has already united himself with Christ; the Christian's body has become a member of Christ and thus is suffused with the Spirit of Christ! "He who cleaves to the Lord is one Spirit with him" (1 Cor. 6:17). In relation to Christ, Christians' bodies are *members;* in relation to the Holy Spirit they are *temples.*

In this text all three persons of the Trinity appear, but Christ is conceived as the "point of physical contact," so to speak, between the Christian and the sanctifying Spirit of God. Note that the term *body* is used here of the physical body of each Christian and not as a technical term for the Church.

The unity theme returns in chapter ten when Paul contrasts pagan idol worship with the Christian Eucharist and insists that Christians are constituted as an entity apart because "the bread we break, is it not a uniting with the body of Christ? Because the bread is one, we, though many, are one body" (1 Cor. 10:16-17). Whereas earlier, the figures used to stress the unity theme were field, building, temple, here for the first time Paul introduces "body" as a term for the community. From "body" as a term for the physical body of the Christian, Paul has now passed to "body" as a term for the Church—and the middle term, the bridge, is the *Eucharistic body* of Christ.

Now the way has been laid for the full development of the Church-Body theme in chapter twelve, where Paul discusses the diversity of functions in the community. "For as the body is one and has many members, and all the members of the body, many as they are, form one body, so also it is with Christist" (1 Cor. 12:12). Notice that for Paul there are not two bodies—the Body of Christ and the body of Christians—but only one. The problem is to explain not how many can be one, but rather, how the one Christ can be many, that is, how the one body of Christ can really have many members. The solution? Paul himself gives it in the following verse: "For in one Spirit we were all *baptized into* one body" (1 Cor. 12:13). Baptism is a grafting of our bodies to the body of Christ (Rom. 6:5), so that now there is really only one body: "Now you are the body of Christ, member for member" (1 Cor 12:27). The unity of Christians is therefore the very unity of Christ; it is created by insertion into the body of Christ in Baptism, and fed and strengthened by the body of Christ in the Eucharist.

We have here a high point in the development of Paul's theology of the indwelling. It is not said that the person of Christ inhabits the Christian, but rather that Christ has become one corporate person by joining Christians in a starkly real and organic way to his own sacred humanity.

In Second Corinthians, to which we now turn, we have an ever greater emphasis on Christ's immanence. Paul never loses the perspective of the Coming Christ, and certainly not in this letter (2 Cor. 1:14) in which he speaks of the heavenly dwelling we look toward, when we will be "at home with the Lord" (2 Cor. 5:8, 10). Nevertheless, in this manifesto of his apostolic career, detailing as it does his hardships and sufferings, the shipwrecks, the stonings, the perils from every side, the hunger and thirst, Paul gives chief stress to the present identification with Christ which all these things effect. "The sufferings of Christ abound in us," he begins (2 Cor. 1:5); we bear the dying of Jesus in our mortal bodies (2 Cor. 4:10). But in all this mystery of suffering and death, the mystery of Christ's risen life is already at work in him; "Always bearing about in our body the dying of Jesus, so that the life also of Jesus may be made manifest in our bodily frame" (2 Cor. 4:10). This is why Paul glories in his infirmities—that the *power of Christ* may *overshadow* him (2 Cor. 12:9). The verb which we here translate "overshadow" is literally, "pitch his tent over," and it evokes God's overshadowing of the meeting tent in the desert and of the

Ark of the Covenant. Here we have the characteristically Israelite idea of the inhabitation as a loving, protective, and manifest presence of divine power. Here Paul comes close to attributing the inhabitation to the person of Christ, but the context shows that he is concentrating more on the manifestation of Christ's power which comes from Paul's identification with the sufferings of Christ.

The immanence of Christ in Second Corinthians does, however, go much deeper than identification with his sufferings on the experiential level. It is rooted in the *new existence* the Christian now enjoys in Christ. To be in Christ means to be *"a new creature"* (2 Cor. 5:17; cf. Gal. 6:15). "Christ Jesus is in you," Paul says (2 Cor. 13:5), and because Christ is, although the outer man undergoes decay, the "inner man is being renewed day by day" (2 Cor. 4:16), and Christians are being transformed into the very image of Christ by Christ himself who energizes them with his transforming Spirit (2 Cor. 3:18).

The temple theme returns in 2 Cor. 6:16 ff. Here Paul is counseling Christians to avoid marriage with unbelievers. Why? Because being in Christ gives Christians a new kind of existence; it sets them apart as day from night (2 Cor. 6:14), making them a proper and exclusive entity, just as the temple of God in the Old Testament was a thing set apart and could bear no trafficking with idols. Now, says St. Paul:

You are the temple of the living God, as God says, "I will dwell and move among them, I will be their God and they shall be my people." Wherefore, "Come out from among them, be separated, says the Lord, and touch not an unclean thing; and I will welcome you in, and will be a Father to you, and you shall be my sons and daughters, says the Lord Almighty" (2 Cor. 6:16-18).

Here again the temple is used as a corporate reality, as an image of the people of God, although certainly the consecration of individual Christians is assumed. And the point is that the divine indwelling which the "in-Christ" consecration effects involves an exclusivity, a being set apart, from which one practical conclusion is that Christians should marry only those who, consecrated in Christ, are subjects of the divine indwelling.

The most impassioned of Paul's letters is the one he wrote to the Galatians. It is in this letter that appears the classical passage: "With Christ I am nailed to the cross. It is now no longer I that live, but Christ lives in me" (Gal. 2:19-20). This text has inspired many mystics, and it has often been taken as an expression of the highest contemplative mysticism on Paul's part, something which only the great saints enjoy and which the ordinary Christian can only aspire to. But this goes patently against the context. Paul is trying to show the Galatians that to cling to the Law when Christ has replaced the Law by fulfilling it, is to cast away the grace of God and to imply that Christ died in vain. To drive the point home in an intensely personal way, Paul begins speaking in the first person. The "I" he uses is not the mystic "I," but what Canon Cerfaux calls the "generic I"—that is, Paul speaks in the person of all Christians inasmuch as they are Christians. The Christian, if he was once a Jew, has "through the Law died to the Law" in order to live for God. Life for him is now found not in the Law but in Christ. And the personal relationship to Christ is one based on faith in the immense act of saving love which was the sacrifice on the cross. Paul no doubt has had a vivid personal experience of what he is saying: Christ living in him by faith. But this is something that should be the normal fortune of anyone who is genuinely Christian and who pays attention to the person of Christ rather than to a host of legal prescriptions.

The long Epistle to the Romans does not add anything substantial to the theology of the indwelling, except that it deepens the sacramental roots of it. Chapters six and seven are especially interesting from this point of view. When we were baptized, Paul says, we grew together [like branches of a tree] into "the likeness of his death," and this means that we shall be with him "in the likeness of his resurrection also" (Rom. 6:5).

As for the indwelling of the divine persons, we have noticed that Paul has never yet used the technical term "indwelling" for Christ himself but only for the Father or the Holy Spirit. Christ has rather been presented as the "point of contact" between his members and the Spirit of God. This is confirmed by Romans 8:9-11, which develops the theology of the indwelling Spirit. Paul here equates two expressions: "Christ in you" and "the Spirit of God *dwelling* in you."

In Colossians, the great themes of Corinthians and Romans are reworked and deepened to stress the headship of Christ over all things (Col. 1:18-20). The thought of the glorious manifestation of Christ at his Second Coming is still strong (Col. 1:22; 3:4), but the stress is on the fact that it is "Christ in you" who is "your hope of glory" (Col. 1:27). The terms "died with Christ" (Col. 2:20), and "risen with Christ" (Col. 3:1), "buried . . . with him," and "also rose" with him (Col. 2:12) are used manifestly of baptism. And Christian life consists in being "rooted in him, built up in him" (Col. 2:7). Colossians advances the theology of the indwelling when Paul says that "all the fullness" of God dwells in Christ (Col. 1:19). Christ himself is a subject of the divine inhabitation, the fullness of the divinity is in him. And a few lines later Paul specifies that the fullness dwells in him *bodily* (Col. 2:9). *Bodily* here means that the indwelling of the

Godhead is in Christ in such a way that it is immediately communicated to his members, joined "bodily" to him. For that is precisely what the sequence
of the text says: "In him dwells all the fullness of the
Godhead bodily, and in him *you* have been filled . . ."
(Col. 2:9-10; italics added).

The point is that, because of his members' organic
union with him, they share in the very quality of
Christ himself as subject of God's indwelling. It seems
only a step—and a legitimate one—to say that Christ
himself indwells his members, but Paul seems to shy
away from saying so, lest his readers lose the grasp
of the starkly real, organic, and as it were *physical*
solidarity effected with Christ's body through baptism
and the Holy Eucharist. That is why he prefers to say
that Christians are *in* Christ, or at most that Christ is *in*
them, without specifying that this is an inhabitation of
the person of Christ. The technical terms for inhabitation are still reserved for the Father and the Holy Spirit.

We now turn to Ephesians, which expresses the final
synthesis of St. Paul. Here the temple theme returns
in the second chapter:

> You are built upon the foundation of the apostles
> and prophets, with Christ Jesus himself as the chief
> corner stone. In him the whole structure is closely fitted
> together and grows into a temple holy in the Lord; in
> him you are being built together into a dwelling place
> for God in the Spirit" (Eph. 2:20-22).

Notice first that this is a Trinitarian text—Father, Son, and Holy Spirit are all specifically named. There is nothing particularly new in this because we have seen them closely associated in other "indwelling" texts. Likewise, here again, it is God or the Spirit of God who indwells. Christ has the physical role once more— here under the image of the corner stone, just as he was in other texts the foundation, or the body to which his members are joined. But what is distinctly new is that the temple appears here not as a static reality but one that is growing. The Church is becoming more and more the subject of divine indwelling. The indwelling is progressive.

To this thought Paul returns in 3:14 ff., a prayer for the growth of the Ephesians. This text combines all the preceding insights with a few new ones, and ties them all together into a magnificent synthesis:

> That is why I bend my knees to the Father . . . from whom all fatherhood in heaven and earth receives its name, that he grant you in a measure in keeping with the riches of his glory, to be strengthened with power through his Spirit unto the progress of your inward man. May Christ find a dwelling place, through faith, in your hearts; may you be rooted, then, and founded in love, so that you may be enabled to grasp, with all the saints, what is the breadth and length and height and depth, and to know Christ's love which surpasses knowledge—in order that you may be filled unto all the fullness of God (Eph. 3:14-19).

First of all this is a prayer—an indication that the gifts of growth Paul asks for are infused by God. The whole object of the prayer is summed up in the Father's bestowal of the Holy Spirit, who will strengthen the Christian and effect his progress. But here is something distinctly new: "May Christ find a dwelling place . . . in your hearts." Not only is a technical term for indwelling now applied for the first time to Christ, but what Paul asks for is a progress in that relationship. If indwelling means consecration, mutual possession, exclusively, and permanence (as we have already seen), what Paul is asking is that Christ, the resident of the heart, deepen all these aspects of his possession of the Christian.

Subjectively speaking, the instrument of this indwelling is faith, to which is joined immediately an ever-firmer charity. Progress, then, in these "theological" virtues, as we call them today, is the measure of the deeper indwelling of Christ. When this happens, the Christian will begin to enjoy the fruit that such a growth is destined to bear: a greater penetration of the mystery of Christ. The dimensions are best interpreted as indicating that the mystery of Christ embraces heaven and earth, Jew and Gentile. The cross is, in the words of St. John Damascene, the "bond of the Universe"— suggesting in the very directions in which it points that it embraces all creation and all men. Realizing how vast, how universal, how ecumenical the mystery is,

Christians will then come to experience what really is beyond expression—the infinite, immeasurable love of Christ (to which his cross testifies), and will, in him, be filled to that fullness of divine life which flows into him from the Father.

It is now safe to say that Christ himself indwells, for the organic aspects of the union of Christians with him seem, to Paul, well enough established. Christ is not only, because of our solidarity with him, the point of contact with divinity. He is himself the indwelling Lord, who comes repeatedly to the soul as if for the first time to make it his own.

The intimacy and directness of the personal union of the Christian with Christ—which our text strongly declares—is still far from impairing the primary meaning of the indwelling as an indwelling in the community. "In your hearts," let us note, here is plural. Faith is the common endowment of all Christians, and charity it is that unites them; and these are the virtues precisely that assure the progressive indwelling of Christ. Moreover, the fruit which is knowledge is not an esoteric thing; the aim of growing faith and love, as of growing inhabitation, is to be able to grasp what all the saints grasp: the cosmic reaches of the cross and the love of Christ to which it testifies.

We can conclude, then, by saying that, although we find a homogeneity in Paul's theology of the indwelling —the basic principles from Damascus to Rome do not change—there is, nevertheless, a refinement and a shift of emphasis. From the horizon of Thessalonians in which Paul conceives the presence of Christ as a coming thing, as the consummation on the last day, he progressively is led to stress his own and the Christian's present union with Christ in experience and in sacrament. He does not call this union with Christ an indwelling. The divine indwelling is referred primarily to the Father and the Holy Spirit. Christians attain this divine indwelling by being joined organically to the humanity of Christ, himself the temple in whom the fullness of the divine presence is realized. This "organic union" with Christ explains, too, why the subject of the divine indwelling is primarily the Christian community, the Church as a corporate reality, for it is the extension of that sacred humanity which is the temple of God. Baptism effects the organic union, the Eucharist perfects it.

Christ does indeed indwell, but this is safe to say only when we have understood that we are organically one with his body, and that this makes us all into a sacred unity. It is important in our day of concern for Christian unity that we return to this humbling realization that God dwells in us primarily as a community and that union with Christ is a corporate and visible reality, and that only in and through that corporate and visible reality do we attain divinity.

Yet, the indwelling of the three divine persons in the body of Christ is not something static and ponderous. It is not meant to inspire complacency in institutionalization, which ultimately spells decay. It is a reality ever to be possessed afresh. The final reunion with Christ, the consummate indwelling, when God will be all-in-all, is prepared for by the progressive indwelling now through firmer faith and deeper love. Would we possess him—or rather be more possessed by him—we need only learn better how to believe and how to love.

6: **FROM WREDE TO THE NEW QUEST: A Sketch of the Background of New Testament Studies** *Von Reimarus zu Wrede* was the title of the original German edition of Albert Schweitzer's book of 1906. It was a book that had a profound effect upon New Testament studies at the time, for it not only summed up much of the work of the last century and noted the various trends, but it also closed an era of New Testament studies and thus itself became an important landmark in that sphere of learning. The idea was to observe what had happened from the publication in 1778 of the work of Reimarus, until the appearance of the work of Wrede in 1901, when, in Schweitzer's view, the wheel of criticism had in some way come full circle. The English translation by William Montgomery of Westminster College, the Presbyterian college of theology in Cambridge, England, appeared in 1910, with the extremely free rendering of the original title: *The Quest of the Historical Jesus;* and with this brilliant choice of terms an important phrase arived in the world of New Testament scholarship.

Hermann Samuel Reimarus (1694-1768) was a teacher of Hebrew in Hamburg, and a classical scholar

whose edition of Dio Cassius earned him esteem in the
learned world of the time. But his most famous work
was withheld from publication until ten years after
his death. This was his *Apologie oder Schutzschrift für
die vernünftigen Verehrer Gottes* ("Apology for the
Rational Worshipers of God"), a defense of the deist
position of pure naturalism, in which all miracles and
mysteries were denied except creation itself, and in
which above all the possibility of revealed religion was
rejected. To be a deist was, for Reimarus, to be a
"rational worshiper of God," that is, to worship God
because he can be discerned from reason, and no more.
This work of Reimarus was considered too alarming
to be published in his lifetime: the whole manuscript,
running to four thousand pages, is said by Schweitzer
to be preserved in the Hamburg municipal library.[1]
Some sections of it, however, were published in 1778
by Gotthold Ephraim Lessing (1729-1781), the drama-
tist and literary critic, who in his later years (from 1770)
as librarian at Wolfenbüttel, near Brunswick, became,
as a deist, much involved in theological controversy,
which became his main preoccupation. These parts of
the work of Reimarus were published anonymously
by Lessing under the title *Wolfenbütteler Fragmente*.
They included essays on the deist position, on the
denial of revelation in the Old Testament, and some

[1] Albert Schweitzer, *The Quest of the Historical Jesus,* trans.
W. Montgomery (New York: Macmillan, 1948), p. 14.

notes on literary criticism of the Pentateuch. Literary criticism of the Bible was at that time in its merest infancy: Astruc had written as recently as 1753, and neither Eichhorn nor Geddes had yet spoken on the subject. But the important fragment for us here is the last to be published by Lessing: *Von dem Zwecke Jesu und seiner Jünger* ("The Aims of Jesus and His Disciples"). For Schweitzer this marks the beginning of modern New Testament studies.

It may be said briefly that the purpose of Reimarus, as a rationalist deist, was the presentation of Jesus as an historical person, freed from all dogmatic preoccupation, and moreover to attempt to distinguish the real historical elements to be found in the Gospels. Schweitzer considered this first attempt of its kind a major landmark: he quotes Reimarus as saying: "We are justified in drawing an absolute distinction between the teaching of the Apostles in their writings and what Jesus himself in his own lifetime proclaimed and taught."[2] In fact this "absolute distinction has continued in New Testament studies up to the present time, in terms of the distinction between *kerygma* and history, and between the "Christ of faith" and the "historical Jesus." It is interesting to find the distinction made as early as 1778. Moreover, Schweitzer was interested to find that, for Reimarus, the central, and perhaps the only, teaching we have from Jesus himself, was an

[2]*Ibid.*, p. 16.

eschatological message, namely, warning of the proximity of the end. Yet, what really concerned Reimarus was to discover the man Jesus in history, distinct from what theology in and after the Gospels has attributed to him.

This attempt marked the beginning of most of the work of the nineteenth century, when scholars were occupied with what came to be called "the quest of the historical Jesus." After publication of the *Fragments* of Reimarus, the public authorities confiscated the edition as subversive to orthodox Christianity and forbade further discussion of it, especially after a controversy between Lessing and the chief pastor of Hamburg, Johann Melchior Goeze (1717-1786), who had attacked Lessing for his impiety in publishing the *Fragments* and had provoked from Lessing some of the most famous and eloquent retorts in the history of theological controversy. But Lessing's publication of Reimarus had done its work, and Schweitzer's book is an account of the history of the "quest" throughout the nineteenth century. The quest passed first through a rationalist stage, reaching eventually to Schleiermacher in 1864, but between 1835 and 1840 the mythical approach of David Friedrich Strauss was being elaborated under the influence of the thought of Hegel. In 1863 appeared Renan's *Vie de Jésus,* again seeking the purely historical Jesus as a foundation for a new view of Christian theology. And about the same time (1850-1852) ap-

peared the completed work of Bruno Bauer, who set out
from an entirely sceptical position and arrived at the
opinion that "there never was any historical Jesus."[3]

Near the end of the century, in 1892, we find a
new and important distinction being brought into this
study by Martin Kähler (1835-1912). The operative
phrase appears in the title of his book: *Der sogenannte
historische Jesus und der geschichtliche, biblische
Christus*, which it is not possible to translate without
explanation. The point lies in the use of the Latin-German
word *Historie*, to indicate an event that happened
but lies buried in the past, and *Geschichte*, the specifically
Germanic word for "history," to indicate something
that happened and is significant. In the climate of the
times, when the "historical Jesus" was being seriously
questioned, the affirmation that something is *Geschichte*
and not *Historie* carries with it the suggestion that the
Christ of *Geschichte*, the Christ that is significant to me,
is all that we have in the Gospel, and not an "historical
Jesus," the Jesus of *Historie* at all. It was Kähler in
1892 who brought the word *kerygma*, or preaching, into
this context: *"The real Christ is the preached Christ,"*[4]
that is, the Christ who is *geschichtlich*, or historically
significant, is the Christ of the *kerygma*; and there is

[3]*Ibid.*, p. 157.
[4]Kähler, 1961 edition, p. 44; cf. Heinz Zahrnt, *The Historical Jesus*, trans. J. S. Bowden (New York: Harper & Row, 1963), p. 83.

an overtone that this is not the same as the Jesus of
Historie. "The real historical figure is the Christ of
preaching and faith because he is historically effective."[5]

It is valuable to notice the origins of these words already before the time of Schweitzer, if only because they
are so frequently used today, without, perhaps, an awareness of their overtones. Thus, many today write "salva-
tion-history" for *Heilsgeschichte*, without being aware
of the connotation of *Geschichte* as opposed to *Historie*,
for the overtones are almost impossible of rendering in
direct translation. And again, *kerygma*, in connection
with *Geschichte* rather than *Historie*, is often used
without awareness of the implications of its use by
Kähler and others since.

And so, after the turn of the century we come to
Wilhelm Wrede (1859-1907), whose book *Das Mes-
siasgeheimnis in den Evangelien* ("The Messianic Secret in the Gospels"), published in 1901, marks for
Albert Schweitzer the end of the Quest. For Wrede,
"The general picture offered by the Gospel is not an
historical representation of the life of Jesus. Only some
faded remnants of such an impression have been taken
over into a suprahistorical religious view."[6] The end of
the quest had been coming since Bauer's sceptical view
in 1850. Here for Schweitzer it had come full circle:
Reimarus had set out to avoid all theological preoccupa-

[5]Zahrnt, *loc. cit.*
[6]Cited in *Quest*, p. 337.

tions and to concentrate on the historical alone: now Wrede had abandoned all historical preoccupations and concentrated on the Christian message, the "messianic secret," incidentally here putting into circulation another phrase that has remained current even among those unaware of the overtones of its division from the historical Jesus. So the quest was at an end. And Schweitzer, too, concentrated on the message: the historical quest was no longer worth pursuing. Schweitzer found himself agreeing with Reimarus, the pioneer of over a hundred years before, that the central element of the message was eschatological, that is, it was teaching men to look forward to the end of all things. And he agreed with Wrede that the ideal of Jesus was infinitely more important than the hopeless pursuit of an historical person: "There is nothing more negative than the result of the critical study of the Life of Jesus,"[7] he wrote near the end of his book: the quest of the historical Jesus had been a failure. But for Schweitzer the message was there, the message that "the end is at hand" remained as the greatest message ever given to mankind, for only thus would mankind prepare for a spiritual renewal. "Jesus means something to our world because a mighty spiritual force streams forth from him and flows through our time also. This fact can neither be shaken nor confirmed by any historical discovery."[8]

[7]Ibid., p. 396.
[8]Ibid., p. 397.

Thus, even if the preaching of Jesus looked forward to a fulfillment that never came, the significance of his preaching *for me* and for all men remained. And even if this involves the supposition that Jesus himself was puzzled, mistaken, or even deluded in his eschatology, the fact remains that this preaching still moves men's hearts. And Albert Schweitzer himself bore witness to the human response to the Christian message when, in his own generous spirit, he chose to throw over everything in his European life to become a medical missionary in Africa, where he worked until he died.

I have elaborated somewhat on the main points of the period from Reimarus to Wrede because many of the elements in the subsequent period, after the declaration of the failure of the quest, have their roots and even their vocabulary in this period.

The first years of the new century were full of developments. In particular there was the so-called *Religionsgeschichtliche schule,* the school of those who approached the problem from the standpoint of comparative religion. One of the chief proponents of this group was Hermann Gunkel (1862-1932), whose book *Zum religionsgeschichtlichen Verständnis des Neuen Testaments* ("Towards an Understanding of the New Testament through the Study of Comparative Religion"), published in 1903, suggests that Christianity is essentially syncretistic, that various religious influences,

Eastern and Western, entered the Christian community after the death of Jesus and endowed his figure with
divine attributes adapted from many other sources. Ten
years later, in 1913, appeared the famous book of
Wilhelm Bousset (1865-1920), *Kyrios Christos*, in
which it was maintained that Jesus after his death
came to be proclaimed *Kyrios* or "Lord" by the Hellenist community in a way analogous to the proclama-
tion in various Hellenist cults of the "Lordship" of
their own deity. This means that, for Bousset, the
cult of Jesus as Lord had completely displaced any
question of an historical Jesus, indicating that the
thought of this school took for granted the abandonment of the quest.

About the same time, Julius Wellhausen (1844-
1918), a devout man and a leader in the study of literary sources in the Old Testament, began to apply that
same method of study to the New Testament. In 1905
he published his *Einleitung in die drei ersten Evangelien* ("Introduction to the First Three Gospels"), which
marks the beginning of modern "source criticism." The
hypothesis of the "Two Sources," Q and Mark, first appeared back in the nineteenth century, but its modern
elaboration began with Wellhausen, who in the same
year produced his *Ur-Marcus*. Hence, the way was paved
towards what became the classical theory for the origin
of the Gospels in B. H. Streeter's *The Four Gospels*
(1924). But theories of fragmentation, when carried

too far, tend to lead to demolition, as happened by 1919 with Karl Ludwig Schmidt's rejection of the Markan framework in *Der Rahmen der Geschichte Jesu* ("The Framework of the History of Jesus").

During the first years of the century there were also two main Catholic reactions to the abandonment of the quest. One was that of Alfred Loisy (1857-1940), with his "petit livre," *L'Évangile et l'Église,* in 1902, and his call for reconciliation of the findings of New Testament criticism with Catholic theology, if need be by the adaptation of Catholic theology to current thought, a notion that caused many to founder amid the storms caused by Modernism. Loisy's book was condemned along with other Modernist writings on the grounds of its denial of permanent dogmatic truth.

The other reaction was expressed in the almost simultaneous publication in 1902 of *La méthode historique,* by Père Marie-Joseph Lagrange, O.P. (1855-1938). Lagrange insisted in his *Historical Method* that the fearless examination of texts and archaeological evidence rendered possible by modern research and scholarship must necessarily guide us to an understanding entirely consonant with the teaching of revelation in orthodox theology. In other words, there could be no abandonment of the quest; on the contrary, difficulties were to be faced squarely even if the evidence at present still leaves their solution far away. And the quest must be pursued by an ever-greater amassing of evidence. We shall see presently that the quest has now taken a slightly different turn from its direction as Lagrange saw it; yet, his principle that sufficient evidence can never lead anywhere but to the truth, and the amount of evidence he amassed, assessed, and placed in historical perspective, avoiding preconceptions not borne out by the historical evidence, remain as a permanent heritage for all scholars. Lagrange's hard work and accumulation of facts have rightly been compared to St. Jerome's. Both men could look fearlessly with the eye of faith and the eye of scholarship.

This brings us to the period after the First World War. Where was the quest going at that time? It was nearly twenty years since others had abandoned it as useless.

By 1919 "source criticism" had threatened the security of the text of the Gospel, and when in that year a new word was placed in currency, many thought that it was going to be the answer. This was in the title of the book *Formgeschichte* by Martin Dibelius in 1919. In English it is usually called *"form criticism,"* although this is not an exact translation of the term used by Dibelius ("form history"). The point of his idea was, of course, that the determination of the literary form of any given passage gives the clue to its historical value. In this way unhistorical "forms" or literary genres, when recognized as such, will not provide historical data. One of the main instruments in determining the "form" was to be the study of the *Sitz im Leben* ("the climate of the times"—literally "the setting in life," or periphrastically, "assessment of the social context"). While there is no doubt whatever about the value of this method, and certain aspects of its application to the Gospels have received general acceptance, there are, inevitably, many areas where opinion is very divided. It is, in fact, a method that must be used in any literary criticism, but we owe its particular application to the study of the Gospels to Martin Dibelius at this time. Yet, form criticism must be kept within proper bounds. It is worth hearing the opinion of the late T. W. Manson on the subject in 1949:

> The term Form Criticism should be reserved for the study of the various units of narrative and teaching which go to make up the Gospels, in respect of their form alone. . . . But Form Criticism got mixed up with two other things. One was K. L. Schmidt's full-scale attack on the Marcan framework; the other was the doctrine of the *Sitz im Leben* . . . [namely] that the Gospels should be studied in their context—so far as we know it—of the interests, problems, and practical needs of the people who first used them. No doubt particular stories and sayings were useful to missionary preachers of the first century: no doubt they gave guidance to the early communities on questions of faith and conduct. But we are travelling much too far and too fast if we infer from that that they were created by

the community to serve these ends or meet these needs.[9]

This warning of Manson is useful here because it serves to introduce one of the greatest names in Protestant theology today, Rudolf Bultmann, who in 1921 published the first edition of his famous book, *Die Geschichte der Synoptischen Tradition* ("The History of the Synoptic Tradition," translated into English in 1963). For in fact it was just such an inference as was indicated by Manson that was made by Bultmann. Manson describes Bultmann's thesis as "an account not of how the life of Jesus produced the tradition, but of how the tradition produced the life of Jesus. And when the work of the tradition has been undone, there is very little of Jesus left."[10] Bultmann took over the basic ideas that we looked at earlier, including Kähler's vocabulary of 1892 with the distinction between significant history, *Geschichte,* and the mere event, *Historie,* and Kähler's use of the word *kerygma* to indicate the tradition as distinct from the historical person. The idea—already advanced by Reimarus—of the "absolute distinction" between what the historical Jesus actually said and what the apostolic writers attributed to him, receives a new vividness from Bultmann, with his distinction between the "Christ of faith" and the "Jesus of history."

[9]T. W. Manson, *Studies in the Gospels and Epistles,* edited by M. Black as a memorial volume to Manson, 1962, pp. 4-6.
[10]*Ibid.,* p. 6.

For Bultmann in 1921 and onwards, the end of the quest twenty years earlier meant that the "Christ of faith" has in the Gospel writings so completely eclipsed the original "Jesus of history" (if there ever was one), as to render the "Jesus of history" quite unattainable. In other words, the Christ of whom we read in the Gospels represents the Christ of faith as understood by the Christians of the first century, and we have in fact no knowledge of how far this corresponds to the Jesus of Nazareth of history. The Christ of faith, for Bultmann, like the *"geschichtlicher Christus"* of Kähler, is the biblical Christ, the Christ of the *kerygma,* the "preached Christ" of Kähler. Thus, Bultmann writes: "It is not the historical Jesus, but Jesus Christ, the Proclaimed One, who is the Lord."[11] It is in fact familiar enough ground when we have been following the eclipse of the "historical Jesus." And it is this situation that was seriously attacked in a broadcast by Professor Donald MacKinnon, an Anglican, and Norris Hulse, Professor of Divinity at Cambridge, entitled "The Bultmann Cul-de-sac" (B.B.C., June 4, 1962), when he said that if we continue this line of distinguishing the Christ of faith and the Jesus of history, the one presented in the *kerygma* and the other unattainable and lost in the past, and perhaps quite insignificant in actual history, as Christian believers we shall soon find

[11]R. Bultmann, *Glauben und Verstehen* (Tübingen, 1933), I, p. 208; cf. Zahrnt, p. 85.

ourselves empty-handed. I listened to this broadcast in
the company of a number of Anglican theological students at Cambridge and witnessed their enthusiastic ap-
plause of the speaker.

Once more we might profitably hear what Manson
said in 1949: "This kind of thing has gone on too long.
. . . What is long overdue is a return to the Gospels
as historical documents. . . . It is necessary to continue the quest of the historical Jesus."[12]

It should be added here, concerning the Gospel of
St. John, that the "Fourth Gospel" had been regarded
as bearing witness to the tradition among Christians
at the end of the first century, and not at all to the
events it purports to relate. But in 1957 Dr. John
Robinson, now Bishop of Woolrich, read a paper
pleasantly entitled "The New Look on the Fourth
Gospel," in which he spoke of the abandonment by
that time of "what might be called the 'critical orthodoxy' [of] the last fifty years . . . still represented in
the most recent commentaries and textbooks," where the
Fourth Evangelist is "not to be regarded, seriously, as a
witness to the Jesus of history, but simply to the Christ
of faith."[13] It continues, of course, to be true that
Protestant textbooks in the majority still conform to the
"critical orthodoxy of the last fifty years," formulated

[12]Manson, *op cit.*, pp. 8, 10.
[13]*Twelve New Testament Studies* (London: SCM Press,
1962), pp. 94, 95.

in terms of the *kerygma,* of the Christ of faith as distinct from the unknown Jesus of history, derived from Kähler of 1892 and Wrede of 1901 and even Reimarus of 1778; they have not yet adverted to the "new look" or the beginnings of the "new quest," which we are about to discuss. And it is rather distressing sometimes to find Catholics being a little out of date and clinging to the same "old look" with its dismissal of the "historical Jesus."

Before we move on to the new quest, we must look at three important movements beginning in the 1930's which contributed to the new situation of today.

The first of these influences of the thirties is that of probably the greatest Protestant theologian of our time, Karl Barth. Although it may be said that Barth has not contributed directly to the solution of the specific problem of the historical Jesus, it is because basically he does not regard this as a problem. Barth is quoted as saying: "In history as such there is nothing as far as the eye can see which can provide a basis for faith."[14] For Barth, the Bible is not man's word about God, or any Christian tradition about Christ: it is God's word to us:

"The Bible tells us not how we should talk with God but what he says to us; not how we should find the way to him, but how he has sought and found the way

[14]Karl Barth, *Epistle to the Romans,* trans. E. Hoskyns (London, 1933); cf. Zahrnt, p. 68.

to us; not the right relation in which we must place ourselves to him, but the covenant which he has made with all who are Abraham's spiritual children and which he has sealed once and for all in Jesus Christ. It is this which is within the Bible. The Word of God is within the Bible.[15]

This "Theology of the Word" of Barth, inspiring men to a response to God's word in the Bible, seems for a time to have led them away and freed them from the anxieties raised by the abandonment of the quest, lifting them up to a "suprahistorical religious view"— to use the words of Wilhelm Wrede in 1901 when Schweitzer saw the quest come to a final end. Hence, although Barth did not contribute directly to pursuit or abandonment of the quest, his thinking profoundly influenced men's attitude towards the problem.

A second element, appearing in 1936, was a contribution to source criticism, which had its beginnings in the world of New Testament studies with Wellhausen in 1905. This is the question of possible Aramaic sources of our Gospels, raised by the American scholar, C. C. Torrey, in 1936 with his *Our Translated Gospels*. The idea was considerably developed in Principal Matthew Black's *An Aramaic Approach to the Gospels and Acts* (1946). The difficulty of the thesis is first of all a linguistic one, the ascertaining of the language current in

[15]Barth, *The Word of God and the Word of Man*, trans. D. Horton (New York: Harper Torchbooks, 1957), p. 43; cf. Zahrnt, p. 70.

the time of Christ; but should the thesis be proved, it would have considerable influence on our notions of the origin of the Gospels, and consequently of their precise value as historical documents, which is the point at which the matter becomes linked with the problem of the historical Jesus.

The third and by far most influential contribution of this period to our present inquiry is a book of permanent importance which in 1936 gave a new turn to the course of New Testament studies: Professor C. H. Dodd's *The Apostolic Preaching and its Developments*. As the title implies, his work is a study of the *kerygma* or primitive Christian preaching, with the suggestion that it is possible to distinguish a central core of teaching, perhaps represented in the early preaching in the Book of Acts, which was the nucleus of the documents that became our Gospels. And Dodd's great contribution here is the idea that this primitive *kerygma* is an outline not only of Christ's teaching or message (and this is now often referred to as *didache* as distinct from *kerygma*), but is an outline that is essentially an historical sketch of his ministry. This is borne out by an examination of Peter's preaching as given in Acts, chapters two to five and especially chapter ten. The supreme importance of this suggestion, in the context of an age which was regarding the *kerygma* of the "Christ of faith" as opposed to any account of the "Jesus of history," or at least carrying a

strong overtone of such an opposition, lies in the affirmation that the *kerygma* is, after all, itself a piece of history.
It was a pupil of Dodd, Professor W. D. Davies of
Union Theological Seminary, New York, who wrote
of him as his "revered teacher" and the one who more
than any other brought about "the change from the
analytic [approach of the form critics] to the synthetic
approach to the New Testament," when he indicated
"a common unifying core . . . the *kerygma* of the primitive community, [which] turned out to be a series of
events—the life, death, and Resurrection of Jesus of
Nazareth."[16] And these remarks come in a chapter
entitled, "A Quest to be Resumed."

And so we approach the end of our inquiry, a review
of events from Wrede, when the old quest was abandoned, to the beginning of the "new quest." During the
nineteenth century, after Reimarus, the historical quest
began, developed, and slowly showed itself by its own
methods to have failed. In the first half of the twentieth
century the trend was away from history in the Gospels,
until Dodd's affirmation of the historical nature of the
kerygma itself. Since then, however, the development
has been vital, although it is still overlooked by many
of the ordinary textbooks and especially the Protestant
commentaries. One of the most important works of the

[16]W. D. Davies, *Christian Origins and Judaism* (Philadel-
phia: Westminster Press, 1962), pp. 3-4.

new movement, a short book but one that can be considered a landmark along with those of Wrede, Schweitzer, and Dodd, is *A New Quest of the Historical Jesus,* published in 1959 by Professor James M. Robinson of the South California School of Theology at Claremont. Building upon Dodd's contention that the primitive preaching was basically historical, Professor Robinson's main thesis is that, in the modern view of history, it is the significance of persons rather than events that is the object of study—and he quotes F. M. Powicke in this connection (p. 30, n.)—and that it is this view of history that must be applied to the Gospels. Then the *kerygma* is seen to be not a falsification nor even an overlaying or eclipsing by tradition of the "historical Jesus," but on the contrary the presentation of a living personality.

We have come to recognize that the objective factual level upon which the nineteenth century operated is only one dimension of history, and that a whole new dimension in the facts, a deeper and more central plane of meaning, had largely been bypassed. The nineteenth century saw the reality of the "historical facts" as consisting largely in names, places, dates, occurences, sequences, causes, effects—things which fall far short of being the actuality of history, if one understands by history the distinctively human, creative, unique, purposeful, which distinguishes man from nature. The dimension in which man actually exists, his "world" . . . the significance he had as the environment of those who knew him, the continuing history his life produces, the possibility of existence which his life presents to me as an alternative—such matters as these have become central in an attempt to understand history. It is this deeper level of the reality of "Jesus of Nazareth as he actually was" which was not reached by "the reconstruction of his biography by means of objective historical method." Consequently, the two meanings of the term "historical Jesus" [in the sense of nineteenth-century historical method and in the sense of history today] no longer coincide.[17]

This means that, while the nineteenth-century quest led, after Wrede and Schweitzer, to the conclusion that the quest was impossible (and Professor James Robinson has a chapter entitled, "The Impossibility and Illegitimacy of the Original Quest"), the New Quest is going ahead on new lines and, far from seeming impossible, by means of a "new look" at the Gospels as historical documents, is beginning once more to look upon the real person of the "historical Jesus." Hence, if we are looking in a history for a living personality, as we do now, in this new sense the Gospels are magnificent history.

In the period of the sixties, since the emergence of the New Quest, a period that has been called "Post Form-Critical" and "Post Kerygmatic,"[18] the teaching of those sometimes named "New Questers" has not been accepted everywhere. The term "Post-Bultmannian" is frequently used to describe those who are continuing

[17]James M. Robinson (London: SCM Press, 1959), pp. 28-29.
[18]*Loc. cit.*

the thought of their master at Marburg. (They are also called the "Marburgers.") In general it may be said that there is a return to the idea of the "historical Jesus," but essentially as freshly understood in existential terms.

One of the principal writers among Post-Bultmannians, Günther Bornkamm, as early as 1956 published his *Jesus von Nazareth* (the very title of which suggests an "historical Jesus"), in which he wrote: "How could faith, of all things, be content with mere tradition, even though it be that contained in the Gospels? It must break through it and seek behind it. . . . It cannot be seriously maintained that the Gospels and their tradition do not allow enquiry after the historical Jesus. Not only do they allow, they demand this effort."[19] At the same time, Bornkamm is insisting that the *kerygma* presents not the "historical Jesus" who lived at a certain time in the past, but "the risen Lord, present with his will, his power, his words." Bultmann himself in 1960, in his *Das Verhältnis der urchristlichen Christusbotschaft zum historischen Jesus* ("Relation of the Primitive Christian Christ-Message to the Historical Jesus"), is now using phrases such as "Christ-Message" and "Christ-Kerygma" with the suggestion that the *kerygma* is presenting Christ himself, living with us and in us, and providing the vital Christian encounter in our lives. Thus, for the Post-Bultmannians, the "historical Jesus"

[19]Günther Bornkamm, *Jesus of Nazareth*, trans. Irene and Fraser McLuskey (N.Y.: Harper, 1960), pp. 9, 22; cf. Zahrnt, p. 96.

only exists historically as the Risen Lord here and now.

Some writers, among them Father Raymond E. Brown, S.S., of Baltimore,[20] view a position like James M. Robinson's as Post-Bultmannian, and use the term "new quest" with reference to the idea of the "historical Jesus" in the sense of the present and existing Risen Lord. Again, it has been said that James Robinson's approach "manifests an existentialist bias."[21]

Is it perhaps possible that the synthesis will lie along the lines of the "new view of history," in which the object of study is the personality and his significance in his own world and in the "continuing history his life produces." In this way perhaps the "new quest" will be able, by reassessment and rethinking, to embrace a wide range of the thought and effort that has been spent by devout and learned people in the search for Jesus. And for us Catholics who can see also with the eye of faith and have the normative guide of doctrine to help us, there is always much to learn from what has been done. None of this work is wasted. The labor spent on textual criticism and on the examination of literary forms, the knowledge of the languages, and the testing of hypotheses—all these contribute to the never-ending quest of the Lord we love and daily serve, who is, who was, and who is to come, and who is the Alpha and Omega, the beginning and the end.

[20]*Catholic Biblical Quarterly*, XXVI (1964), p. 4.
[21]*Ibid.*, p. 165, n.

INDEX OF PROPER NAMES